NEW iLearn ENGLISH

3

Student's Book

Gisele Aga
Patricia McKay Aronis
Renata Chimim
Tatiana Martin

Pearson

MISTO
Papel | Apoiando o manejo florestal responsável
FSC® C103535

The publisher would like to thank the following for their kind permission to reproduce their photographs:

123rt: 38; **Acervo Pearson**, Martin Luther King, **p. 1, Penguin Readers:** 140; Alamy: 72, 78, 142; **Dreamstime:** 14, 18, 32, 46, 50, 63, 72, 71, 77, 84, 91, 102, 104, 105, 106, 138, 143, 147, 165, 170; **Garfieldcollectibles.com:** 170; **Getty Images:** 77, 84, 115; **Gocomics,**
***Peanuts*:** 178; **Istock:** 8, 9, 10, 11, 12, 16, 18, 23, 24, 26, 27, 28, 31, 32, 34, 35, 36, 37, 38, 39, 41, 42, 44, 45, 46, 48, 49, 50, 52, 54, 56, 57, 58, 61, 64, 68, 69, 71, 72, 74, 78, 80, 82, 83, 85, 86, 87, 88, 91, 93, 96, 97, 98, 99, 100, 101, 106, 110, 111, 112, 113, 114, 117, 118, 119, 120, 122, 123, 124, 125, 128, 129, 131, 132, 136, 137, 138, 139, 141, 143, 146, 148, 151, 150, 149, 151, 152, 153, 155, 156, 158, 159, 160, 161, 162, 164, 165, 166, 167, 168, 169, 170, 172, 173, 174, 176, 177, 179;
***O Estado de S. Paulo*:** 86; **Shutterstock:** 10, 18, 31, 34, 37, 63, 76, 77, 78, 84, 85, 91, 97, 170, 171, 174; **Theteacherscorner.net:** 70

Illustrations

Shutterstock: 174; **Dreamstime:** 174; **Istock:** 13, 16, 18, 19, 40, 46, 48, 54, 55, 56, 70, 72, 97, 107, 139, 154, 156, 171, 179

Printed in Brazil by Reproset RPPA 222127

NEW iLearn ENGLISH

3

Student's Book

Contents

Presentation

Student's Book

The *New iLearn English* uses the PPP learning methodology. In the **Presentation** stage new structures are presented, in the **Practice** stage students will practice the new structures by means of controlled activities and with more interference from the teacher, so that during the **Production** stage they can use these structures for more spontaneous communication.

Opening Pages

Every unit starts with two Opening Pages containing:

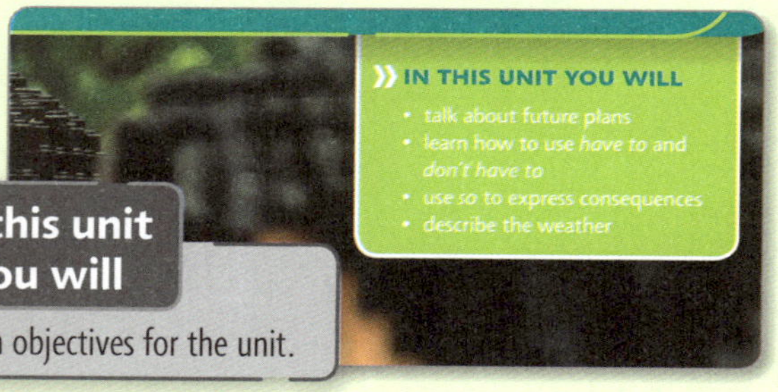

In this unit you will

Main objectives for the unit.

Start up

Warm-up activity for content contextualization.

P LOADING

Section for the **Presentation Stage**

P UPLOADING

Section for the **Practice Stage**

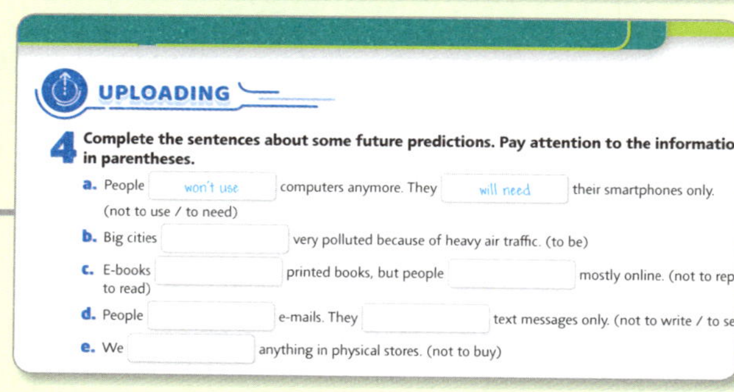

P DOWNLOADING

Section for the **Production Stage**

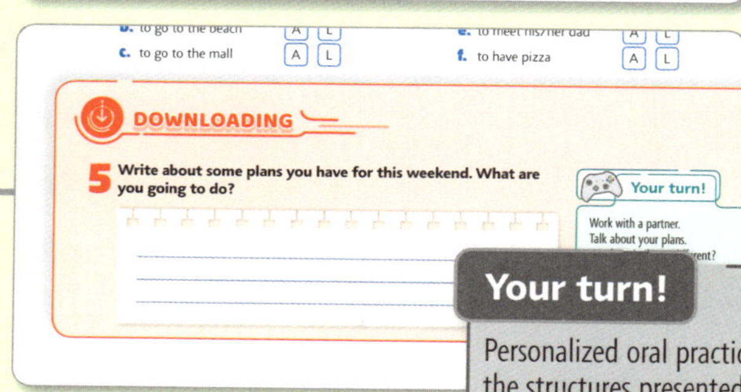

Your turn!

Personalized oral practice of the structures presented.

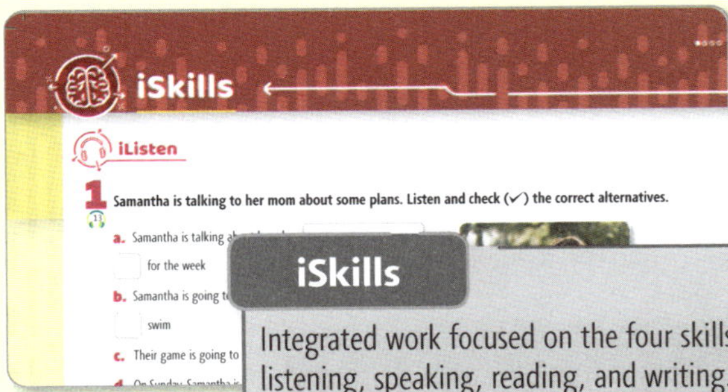

iSkills

Integrated work focused on the four skills: listening, speaking, reading, and writing.

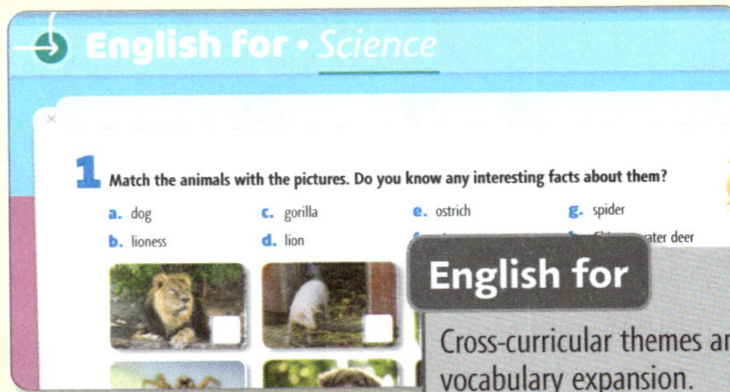

English for

Cross-curricular themes and vocabulary expansion.

rePlay

Revision of grammatical and lexical structures in a fun way.

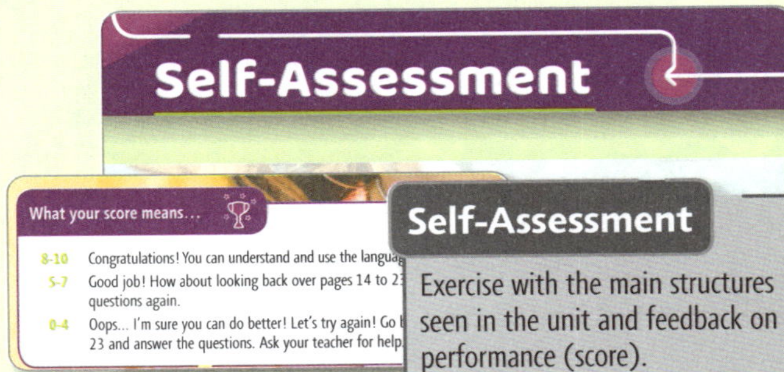

Self-Assessment

Exercise with the main structures seen in the unit and feedback on performance (score).

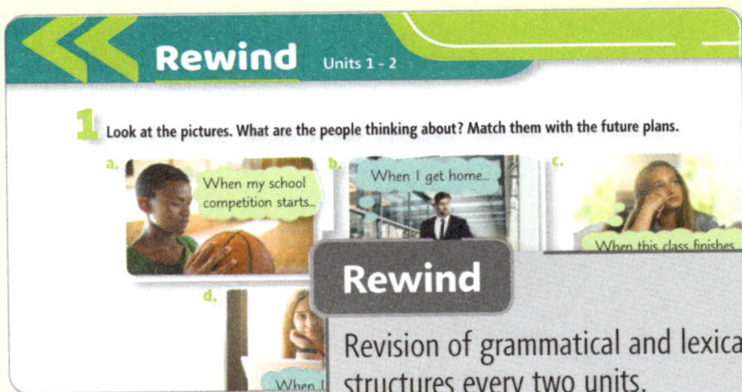

Rewind

Revision of grammatical and lexical structures every two units.

Reading Hub

Extra reading activities with revision of grammatical and lexical structures in a fun way.

Workbook

Grammar Reference

Self-study guide for each unit.

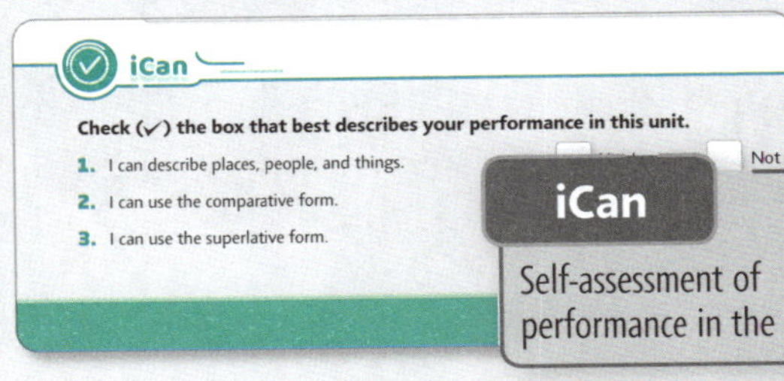

iCan

Self-assessment of performance in the unit.

Digital Components

Pearson English Portal - Exclusive teacher and student areas for extra resources, including tests, audio, and e-books.

Welcome Unit

IN THIS UNIT YOU WILL

- compare the uses of the Present Continuous and the Simple Present
- compare the use of *can* and *can't* for permission and ability
- talk about musical instruments

START UP

Let's plug in! What do you usually do on Mondays?

LOADING

1 Mateus is usually very busy. Today he is telling his classmates about his routine. Listen to what he usually does on Mondays. Is anything similar to your routine?

02

2 Now listen again and complete the paragraph about Mateus.

03

On Mondays Mateus ______ at 6:00 o'clock and ______ his bike to school. School ______ at 3:00 p.m. and he ______ to acting class. At 7:00 p.m. he ______ his mom with dinner. After dinner he ______ video game or ______ TV.

3 Today is Monday, but it's a public holiday. Mateus and his friends don't have classes. Look at what they are doing today and complete the sentences.

to skateboard | to text | to ride | to play

Mateus

Carlos

Clarissa and Bia

Bruna

a. Mateus is riding a bike to the park.

b. Carlos and his father ______ chess.

c. Clarissa and Bia ______ .

d. Bruna ______ on her phone.

UPLOADING

4 Read the sentences and circle the correct option.

a. My sister **is having / has** drama classes at school at the moment.
b. Listen! Mateus **is singing / sings** in his bedroom.
c. I **am having / have** acting classes on Mondays.
d. In this picture, my mom and dad **are having / have** dinner in a Chinese restaurant.
e. Maya **is studying / studies** in the afternoon.

Grammar feed

Simple Present vs. Present Continuous

Carlos **doesn't play** chess at school every day.
He **always plays** chess at home.

X

Today is a holiday and Mateus **isn't riding** his bike to school.
He **is riding** his bike to the park now.

5 Write sentences about these people. Follow the model.

	... every day.	... now.
a. Tina	to take a shower	to take a bath
b. Matt	to text his friends	not to use his phone
c. My parents	to read the newspaper	to watch a sitcom
d. I	to surf the web	to study English

a. Tina takes a shower every day, but she is taking a bath now.
b.
c.
d.

DOWNLOADING

6 Write two sentences about your routine and two sentences about what two people in your family are doing now. Talk to a classmate and compare your sentences.

LOADING

1 **The 8th graders at Riverside School are forming a band. Listen to the sounds and match them with the instruments.**

04

☐ piano	☐ drums	☐ bass
☐ guitar	☐ tambourine	☐ electric guitar

2 **Now match the instruments with the pictures.**

☐

☐

☐

☐

☐

☐

3 **Meg is talking to her mom about the Riverside School Band. Listen and read.**

05

Meg: Hey, Mom, you know…
Mother: Yes?
Meg: Carla can play the piano really well.
Mother: Really? That's nice.
Meg: Yes, and Gabriel can play the drums.
Mother: Are they in your school band?
Meg: Yes, they are.

06

Meg: Can I go to Felipe's house?
Mother: No, you can't. You have to do your homework.
Meg: Oh, but today we want to practice for the show.
Mother: I'm sorry, but not today. You can practice tomorrow.

Study this

She plays **the** piano. They play **the** tambourine.

Grammar feed

Asking for permission: *Can*

A: Can I go to Felipe's house?
B: No, you can't.

vs.

Ability: *Can*

Carla can play the piano and Gabriel can play the drums.

UPLOADING

4 **Read the sentences and pay attention to the words in bold. Then write *P* for *permission* and *A* for *ability*.**

a. My cousin **can play** the guitar very well. ☐

b. I **can't play** in the band today because I have to study. ☐

c. **Can** I **come** in? ☐

d. **Can** you **play** a musical instrument? ☐

DOWNLOADING

5 **You and your classmates are going to form a band. Interview three classmates and take notes in the chart below.**

A: Can you play a musical instrument?

B: ______

A: What musical instrument can you play?

B: ______

CLASSMATE	

6 **Imagine you are a teacher. Look at the class contract and put "✓" next to the activities that are permitted and "X" next to the activities that are not permitted.**

Class Contract

- to eat and drink in the classroom ☐
- to play games on my cell phone ☐
- to go to the restroom ☐
- to do exercises with classmates ☐
- to answer the tests in pencil ☐
- to come in late ☐
- to chew gum ☐

Your turn!

Work with a partner.

He/She is a new student in your class. Answer his/her questions about the contract. Then switch roles.

Can I chew gum in class?

Yes, you can.
or
No, you can't.

unit 1

We're going to see an exhibition.

IN THIS UNIT YOU WILL

- talk about future plans
- learn how to use *have to* and *don't have to*
- use *so* to express consequences
- describe the weather

START UP

Let's plug in!
What are your plans for the weekend?

LOADING

1 **Daniel and Mariela are chatting about what they are going to do on the weekend. Listen and read.**

07

Daniel: So... what are you going to do this weekend?
Mariela: It's my grandma's 80th birthday so we're going to celebrate with her!
Daniel: Wow!
Mariela: She's the best!
Daniel: How are you going to celebrate?
Mariela: We're going to have a big party with my family and some friends. I'm going to help my mom cook a traditional Mexican meal.
Daniel: That's nice! I didn't know you could cook.
Mariela: Of course I can! What about you? What are you going to do?
Daniel: On Saturday I'm going to study for the geography test and on Sunday my family and I are going to see an exhibition.
Mariela: Really? What kind of exhibition are you going to see?
Daniel: It's a Lego exhibition.
Mariela: Are you going to see *The Art of the Brick*?
Daniel: Yes!
Mariela: That's so cool! Talk to you next week then. Bye, Dan.
Daniel: Have fun! Bye.

2 **Read the dialogue again and answer the questions.**

a. Who is going to see an art exhibition? ____
b. Who is going to a special celebration? ____
c. Who is going to cook a traditional meal? ____
d. Who is going to study for a test? ____

UPLOADING

Grammar feed

Questions	Statements
	Affirmative
What **is** Daniel **going to do** on Saturday?	He**'s going to study** for the geography test. Mariella **is going to celebrate** her grandma's birthday.
	Negative
Are Daniel and his family **going to see** an art exhibition on Saturday?	No, they **aren't**. Mariela **is not going to** see an art exhibition.

3 **Use the prompts to write questions with *be going to*. Then match the questions with the answers.**

a. John / play on the school soccer team / this year

Is John going to play on the school soccer team this year?

b. What / Jake and Tom / do on their vacation

______

c. When / Clara / take ENEM

______

d. Kayla / visit her grandparents / in July

______

[ ] They're going to do volunteer work.

[a] No, he isn't. He's going to play on the basketball team.

[ ] She's going to take it in October.

[ ] Yes, she is. She visits them every year.

4 **Listen to Anderson and Laura talking about their plans for Saturday. Circle *A* for *Anderson's* plans and *L* for *Laura's*.**

08

a. to study for a test A L

b. to go to the beach A L

c. to go to the mall A L

d. to visit Grandma A L

e. to meet his/her dad A L

f. to have a pizza A L

DOWNLOADING

5 **Write about some plans you have for this weekend. What are you going to do?**

______

______

______

Your turn!

Work with a partner. Talk about your plans. Are they similar or different?

LEARNING STRATEGY

LOADING

1 **Look at what Daniel and some of his school friends are going to do on their vacation. Listen and repeat the activities.**

09

a.

Go rafting on the Pacuare River in San José, Costa Rica.

b.

Ride the Sugarloaf Mountain cable car in Rio de Janeiro, Brazil.

c.

Swim with whale sharks in Cancun, Mexico.

d.

Watch the dolphins in South Carolina, the U.S.A.

2 **Go back to the sentences in Activity 1 and answer these questions.**

a. Where is Daniel going to travel to?

He is going to travel to Costa Rica.

b. What is Beatriz going to do in Brazil?

c. What is Chris going to do in Cancun?

d. Where is Ryan going to watch the dolphins?

Grammar feed

Future: *Be going to*

Questions

A: What **are** you **going to do** on your vacation?

B: I**'m going to swim** with whale sharks in Cancun.

C: We**'re not going to travel anywhere**. We're **going to stay** at home.

A: Is Chris **going to** Cancun?

B: Yes, he **is**.

A: Is Beatriz **going to** Costa Rica?

B: No, she **isn't**. She **is going to** Brazil.

UPLOADING

3 **Write complete sentences about future plans. Use *be going to*.**

a. John / visit his grandparents / on the weekend

John is going to visit his grandparents on the weekend.

b. I / move to Belo Horizonte / next month

c. She / read a lot / during winter break

d. He / sleep late / on Sunday

e. Akira and his family / travel to Japan / in the summer

f. They / make cupcakes / tonight

DOWNLOADING

4 **Work with a partner. Look at what Guto's cousins are going to do in January. Complete the last card with information about yourself.**

Taís
What: travel to Florianópolis
Who: family
Where: a luxury hotel
How long: six days

Erik
What: go camping in the mountains
Who: friends
Where: campsite
How long: one week

Me
What:
Who:
Where:
How long:

Your turn!

Take turns asking and answering questions about Guto's cousins' vacation plans. Use the dialogue below as a model.

A: What is Taís going to do in January?
B: She's going to travel to Florianópolis.
A: Cool.
B: Who is going to travel with her?
A:
A: Great! Where is she going to stay?
B:
A: And how long is she going to stay there?
B:

LOADING

1 **These teens are asking permission to do something. Listen and read.**

10

a.

b.

2 **Read the comic strips again. Circle the correct alternatives.**

a. Sam wants to	go to Felipe's house.	clean his room.
b. Sam's mother says he needs to	go to Felipe's house.	clean his room.
c. Sam doesn't have to	go to school today.	clean his room.
d. Diana wants to	get a book from the Reading Corner.	finish her test.
e. Mr. Silva says she needs to	get a book from the Reading Corner.	finish her test.

3 **Listen again and repeat the dialogues.**

11

UPLOADING

Grammar feed

Obligation: *Have to*

It's an obligation.

I **have to finish** the test before getting a book from the Reading Corner.

Sam **has to clean** his room before playing video games with Felipe.

It's not an obligation.

We **don't have to go** to school today.

Diana **doesn't have to read** a book.

4 **Look at the pictures. Then complete the dialogues with the correct form of *have to*.**

a.

Lucia: Ms. Taylor, can I go to the restroom?

Ms. Taylor: Yes, you can. But you have to finish the exercises when you come back.

Lucia: OK, thanks.

b.

Ben: Can I borrow your history notes, Laura?

Laura: Sorry, I need them because I ________ study for the test tomorrow. But why don't we study together?

Ben: Great, Laura! Thanks!

c.

Jared: Paula is still watching TV. Doesn't she ________ get up early tomorrow?

Katya: No, she doesn't. Tomorrow is Saturday. She can sleep in the morning. She only ________ go to ballet class after lunch.

DOWNLOADING

5 **Think of your obligations at home and at school. Write two things you *have to* do and two things you *don't have to* do.**

I have to...

a. ________

b. ________

I don't have to...

a. ________

b. ________

Your turn!

Work in groups of three. Compare your sentences. Do you have similar obligations?

LOADING

1 **Listen and read the dialogues.**

12 **a.**

b.

2 **Read the dialogues again and circle the correct alternatives.**

a. **It is/It is not** raining hard in picture ***a***.

b. Tom is upset because he **can/can't** play soccer.

c. It is **cloudy/sunny** in picture ***b***.

d. Luisa is going to play basketball **outside/inside**.

Grammar feed

***So* for consequences**

Michael's last math test score was awful, **so** he is having extra classes this week.

result or consequence

UPLOADING

3 **Match the columns.**

a. It is raining hard,

b. The weather is fantastic outside,

c. It is cold in here,

[ ] so let's put on our coats.

[ ] so we can't leave now.

[ ] so let's go to the beach.

4 **Look at the pictures and complete the sentences about people in the U.S.A. with *so* and the phrases from the box.**

people can ride their bikes outdoors ~~people do activities outdoors~~
the trees turn red and brown people stay in and enjoy hot drinks

a.

It's summer, so people do activities outdoors.

b.

It's fall, ______

c.

It's spring, ______

d.

It's winter, ______

DOWNLOADING

5 **What's your favorite season: summer, winter, spring, or fall?** ______

Invite your friends to do something with you. Use *Let's...*

______

______

iListen

1 **Samantha is talking to her mom about some plans. Listen and check (✓) the correct alternatives.**

13

a. Samantha is talking about her plans ________.
- [ ] for the week
- [ ] for the weekend

b. Samantha is going to ________ on Saturday morning.
- [ ] swim
- [ ] play basketball

c. Their game is going to be on ________.
- [ ] Monday
- [ ] Sunday

d. On Sunday, Samantha is going to ________.
- [ ] have fun with her family
- [ ] go out with her friends

e. Samantha's mother is going to prepare ________.
- [ ] some ice cream
- [ ] a picnic

iWrite

2 **What are your plans for the weekend? Write.**

16:29

	Saturday	Sunday
morning		
afternoon		
evening		

iSpeak

3 **Think of some plans you have for your dream vacation. Write them down.**

a. Where? ________

b. When? ________

c. How to get there? ________

d. What to do there? ________

Now, work with a partner. Talk to him/her about your plans. Then switch roles. Are your plans similar?

1 **Discuss these questions with your teacher and classmates.**

a. Do you visit museums? Why (not)?

b. When you decide to visit a museum, do you look for information about it first?

c. What kind of information is usually available online for visitors?

iThink

2 **Read the information the National Museum of Cambodia offers for visitors on their website and check your predictions.**

READING STRATEGY

INFORMATION FOR VISITORS

The National Museum of Cambodia is situated on 13th Street in the center of Phnom Penh, adjacent to the Royal Palace. Visitors can enter the museum compound and buy admission tickets at the corner of 13th and 178th Street. The museum is open daily from 8:00 a.m. to 5:00 p.m., with the last tickets sold at 4:30 p.m.

Admission fees are based on age and nationality. Foreign visitors aged 10 to 17 years old are charged $5, while those over 18 years old pay $10. Cambodian nationals pay a nominal fee of 500 riels. Entrance is free for children and school groups.

Guided tours can be arranged at the museum entrance for both individuals and groups, and are available in Khmer, English, French, and Japanese.

While photography is not allowed inside the museum galleries, visitors are welcome to film or photograph the museum's exterior and courtyard. Those who wish to get images of the museum or its collection for academic or publication purposes should email the museum to ask for an application form or contact a staff member.

The museum store, located at the main entrance, offers a variety of items for sale, including postcards, souvenirs, replica sculptures, and books on various art and culture topics.

3 **Read the text again and answer the questions**

see word pop-up page 150

a. Where is the visitor's entrance located?

It's on the corner of 13th and 178th Street.

b. What time does the museum open?

c. Is it possible to buy tickets at 5 p.m.?

d. How much do children and school groups pay?

e. Can we take photos inside the museum?

f. What can we buy at the museum store?

project

rePlay

1 Look at the picture for two minutes. Choose two people, memorize as much information as you can about them, and then close your books.

2 Work in pairs. Tell your partner what the people you chose in the picture are going to do. Switch roles. Your partner talks about two other people.

3 What do they have to do? Choose a phrase from the box and write.

to clean their room | ~~to wash the dishes~~ | to finish (his/her) math exercises | to go to school

a.

Pedro has to wash the dishes.

b.

Alana

c.

The boys

d.

Janaína

Self-Assessment

Circle the correct option to complete the sentences.

1. What are you going **to do/do**?
2. What kind of exhibition are you **going to visit/go visit**?
3. Mariela is cold **so/but** she is going to put on a jacket.
4. **A:** Is John going to play on the school soccer team this year?
   B: Yes, **he is going/he is**.
5. **A:** When is Carla going to take the test?
   B: Yes, she is./She's going to take it tomorrow.
6. You **have/has** to clean your room first.
7. Our school competition **is/are** going to start on Monday.
8. She has to **study for the test/watch TV** to get good grades.
9. She **hasn't to/doesn't have to** go to school today.
10. It's summer so let's **stay home and drink some hot chocolate/go to the beach**.

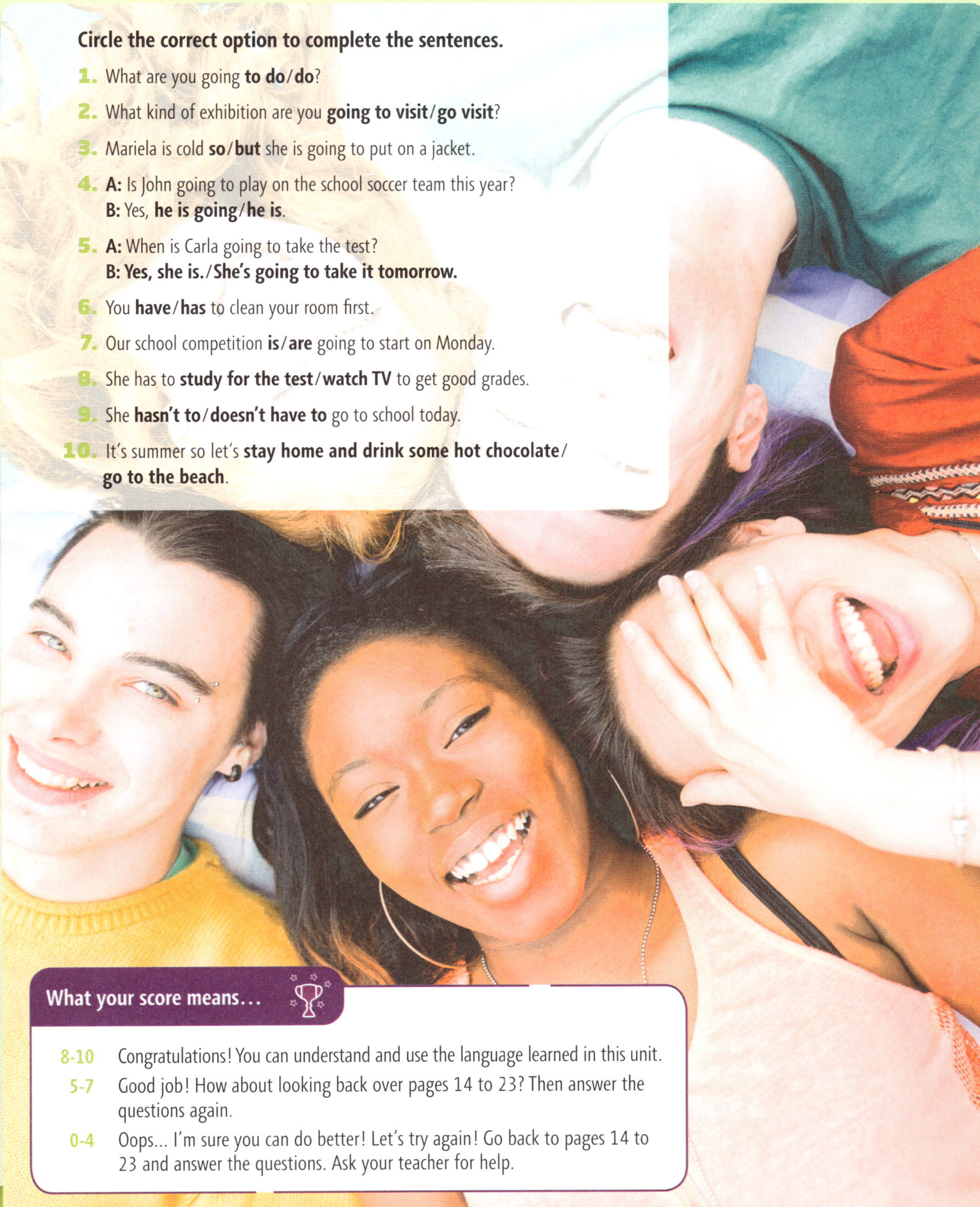

What your score means...

- 8-10 Congratulations! You can understand and use the language learned in this unit.
- 5-7 Good job! How about looking back over pages 14 to 23? Then answer the questions again.
- 0-4 Oops... I'm sure you can do better! Let's try again! Go back to pages 14 to 23 and answer the questions. Ask your teacher for help.

unit 2

Will things be different then?

IN THIS UNIT YOU WILL

- make predictions about the future
- talk about immediate decisions
- make future plans
- discuss the difference between *be going to* and *will*

START UP

Let's plug in! What can you see in the picture? Are there any similarities between the picture and the place where you live? Do you think the world will be like that in the future? Explain.

LOADING

1 **It is 7:30 in the morning. Some students are in the classroom, waiting for their teacher to come in. Listen and read their conversation.**

14

2 **Read the dialogues again. Then decide if the sentences are T (true) or F (false).**

see word pop-up page 154

a. Ethan will help Aiden do the exercise. T F

b. Noah will close the window. T F

c. Emma will have a party at her house. T F

d. Ava will bring some soda. T F

3 **Listen again and repeat the dialogues.**

15

Grammar feed

Spontaneous decisions and offers: *Will*

Fact		Decision
It's very hot in here!	→	I'll open the window.
Let's have a party!	→	I'll bring some soda.

UPLOADING

4 **Match the facts in the pictures with the decisions. Then complete the sentences with *will* and the verb in parentheses. Use contractions.**

a.

Let's go to the movies tonight.

c.

Ryan's grades are low, Mr. Johnson.

b.

It's very hot in here.

d.

Thiago is late for the concert.

[c] Thanks, Ms. Spencer. I ['ll talk] to him and offer to help with his homework. (to talk)

[ ] We [ ] for him and eat our popcorn! (to wait)

[ ] I [ ] the window. (to open)

[ ] Great idea! I [ ] my mom to buy the tickets online right now. (to ask)

5 **Listen to the dialogues. Do they express predictions or decisions? Write *P* for *predictions* or *D* for *decisions*.**

16 **a.** [ ] **b.** [ ] **c.** [ ] **d.** [ ]

DOWNLOADING

6 **Think of two situations you need help with and write them down.**

a. I'm hungry.

b.

c.

Your turn!

Work with a partner. Talk to him/her about your situations. Your partner then offers to help you.

a. I'll get you something to eat.

b.

c.

LOADING

1 Jacob and Benjamin are talking about schools in the future. Read and listen.

17

Jacob: Will schools be different in the year 3000?

Benjamin: Of course! They will be very different from the way they are now. I don't think students will go to school anymore. They'll learn at home.

Jacob: Do you really think so?

Benjamin: Yeah. Teachers will be at schools, but they'll have only online contact with students.

Jacob: But what about the friends we make at school? How will we make friends then?

Benjamin: Online! We already do that, don't we? We don't need to leave home to make friends.

Jacob: Well, I don't. But I'm not sure I like this future…

2 Read the dialogue again and complete the sentences.

a. Benjamin thinks schools [will be] very different in the year 3000.

b. In Benjamin's opinion, [ ] won't go to school anymore.

c. He also thinks teachers will have contact with students [ ] only.

d. Benjamin makes [ ] online.

3 Listen again and repeat the dialogue.

18

Grammar feed

Predictions about the future: *Will*

Statements		Questions
Affirmative	Schools **will be** very different in the year 3000. Students **will learn** at home.	**Will** schools **be** different in the year 3000? **Yes**, they **will**. / **No**, they **won't**.
Negative	Teachers **won't see** students in person. We **won't leave** home to make friends.	How **will** we **make** friends in the year 3000? We**'ll make** friends online.

UPLOADING

4 **Complete the sentences about some future predictions. Pay attention to the information in parentheses.**

a. People [won't use] computers anymore. They [will need] their smartphones only. (not to use / to need)

b. Big cities [ ] very polluted because of heavy air traffic. (to be)

c. E-books [ ] printed books, but people [ ] mostly online. (not to replace / to read)

d. People [ ] e-mails. They [ ] text messages only. (not to write / to send)

e. We [ ] anything in physical stores. (not to buy)

5 **Order the words to form sentences.**

a. time - arrive - we - on - won't

b. only - electric - will - cars - we - use

c. eat - will - organic - everybody - food - only

DOWNLOADING

6 **Use the prompts to write your own predictions for the year 3000. Use *will* or *won't*.**

a. Robots

Robots will feed our pets. / Robots won't feed our pets.

b. Cars and motorcycles

c. The climate

d. Cities

Your turn!

Work with a partner. Compare your predictions. Are they the same or different?

In my opinion, robots will feed our pets in the year 3000.

Well, in my opinion, robots won't feed our pets in the year 3000.

LOADING

1 **Read and listen to these conversations.**

19 **a.**

b.

c.

2 **Read the conversations again. Underline the correct alternatives.**

a. Mason is packing because he is going away for the **holiday/weekend**.
b. Charlotte is going to **ride a bike/sell her bike**.
c. Dad is going to **make a birthday cake/buy a birthday cake**.

3 **Listen again and repeat the dialogues.**

20

Grammar feed

Future Plans: *Be going to*

Statements		**Questions**
Affirmative	I'**m going to** camp out in the mountains for the holiday. I'**m going to** sell my bike.	**Are** you **going to** make Mom's birthday cake, Dad? Yes, **I am.**/No, **I'm not.**
Negative	I'**m not going to** make a cake this year.	Why **are** you **going to** do that? Because this bike is too small for me now.

UPLOADING

4 **Here are the plans of some members of a family for the weekend. Match the columns and write sentences with *be going to*.**

a. Abigail / to study | ☐ the flowers
b. Abigail and Max / to water | ☐ them with their homework
c. Abigail / to fix | a for the final exam
d. Granny Spencer / to help | ☐ a new car
e. Max / to spend | ☐ her bike
f. Ms. Spencer / get | ☐ two hours studying

a. Abigail is going to study for the final exam (on the weekend).
b.
c.
d.
e.
f.

5 **What is going to happen? Use the verbs from the box and write about the pictures.**

to drive — ~~to have~~ — to play

a.
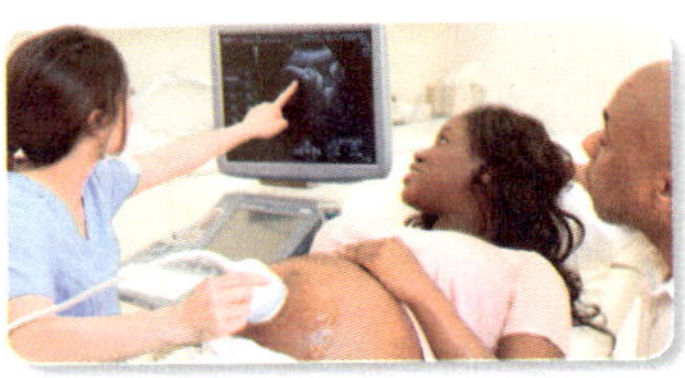
She is going to have a baby.

b.

c.

DOWNLOADING

6 **Think of the plans some members of your family have for tomorrow. Write about them. Share your sentences with a classmate.**

a.
b.

LOADING

1 **Look at these pictures and read the dialogues.**

a.

b.

c.

2 **Read the dialogues again and check the correct alternatives.**

a. Isabella and her friend are sure it's going to rain. ☐

b. The little girl decides to have cereal for breakfast. ☐

c. The boy's family plans to visit South Africa. ☐

Grammar feed

Future: *Be going to* vs. *Will*

Everything **is going to be** different next year, I promise.
It's **going to** rain.

A future action that emphasizes a present intention, certainty, or plan.

Everything **will** probably **be** different next year.
I'**ll have** some pancakes.

A future action that is a spontaneous decision, offer, or prediction.

UPLOADING

3 **Circle the correct alternatives.**

a. I think our history test tomorrow **will be/is going to be** difficult.
b. I **am going to play/will play** tennis with Ian on Saturday.
c. Those boxes look heavy! I **will help/am going to help** you carry them.
d. We **will have/are going to have** lunch with our teachers on Teachers' Day.

4 **Complete the sentences with the verbs in parentheses and the correct form of *be going to* or *will*.**

a.

c.

b.

d.

DOWNLOADING

LEARNING STRATEGY

5 **Work in groups. Write a sentence for each picture below and create a short story. Use *be going to* or *will*.**

______
______
______
______
______

iSkills

iListen

1 Listen to some people who need help in different situations and number the pictures according to the situations you hear.

21

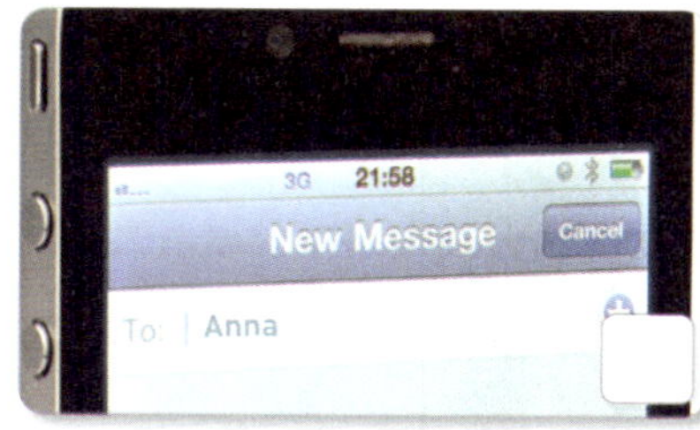

iSpeak

2 Work in pairs. Read these situations and make sentences about the future using *be going to* or *will*.

This text is really difficult.

There's a new adventure movie on.

The bell is ringing, but I can't open the door.

Your grades aren't very good.

Look at those black clouds!

He is walking toward a high cliff.

iWrite

3 What do you think schools will be like in the year 3000? Write about it, then share your thoughts with your teacher and classmates.

English for • *Citizenship*

1 What kind of volunteer work do you know? In your opinion, what are the benefits of being a volunteer?

iThink

2 Read this text from a senior living community website in Connecticut, the U.S.A. What are the benefis of volunteering according to the text?

The Advantages of Volunteering with Older Adults

In today's busy world, making time to volunteer can be hard, but it's very rewarding. If you're interested in volunteering but aren't sure where to start, think about helping out at a local senior living community or senior center.

Volunteering with older adults not only allows you to give back, but you can also gain a lot personally. It can make a big difference in the lives of the seniors you help, in your community, and in your own life as well.

Why Senior Citizens?

Older adults deal with many challenges because of the aging process, such as physical difficulties and changes in thinking abilities. However, they still have much to offer. Helping out with seniors gives you a great chance to learn from them and build meaningful relationships.

If you're holding back from volunteering with seniors because you're unsure about what to expect, here are a few helpful tips:

- Many seniors struggle with loneliness and simply want companionship, especially if their family members are separated from them by location or time constraints.
- When you volunteer, you might just need to sit and chat, listen to their stories, or join them in a simple activity like a craft or board game. Activities like playing cards, walking, gardening, or baking can spark conversations, build relationships, and create both old and new memories.
- It's a common myth that aging adults have lost a desire to learn new things. While this may be true for some, many seniors are eager to learn, especially about technology. If you enjoy tech, you can help a senior learn to use a computer or tablet.

3 Match some words from the text to their meanings.

see word pop-up page 154

READING STRATEGY

project

a. aging	☐	something that limits your freedom to do what you want
b. constraints	☐	to obtain or achieve something you want or need
c. desire	☐	a strong hope or wish
d. to gain	☐	the state of being unhappy because you are alone or do not have anyone to talk to
e. to hold back	☐	becoming old
f. loneliness	☐	to make someone or something stop moving forward

Definitions by Longman Dictionary of Contemporary English

1 Create a time capsule.

A time capsule is a container preserving articles and records of our present day for study by scientists in the distant future.

a. Work with a partner. Agree on five predictions you think will happen, write them down, and put in the time capsule. Imagine that scientists will open it in the year 3000!

b. Your choices should reflect our lifestyles right now. Your teacher can help you with words you do not know.

c. Now work with another pair of students and compare your time capsules. Do you have similar predictions?

2 New Year's Resolutions!

Imagine it's New Year's Eve and you are making resolutions. Think of 5 plans you have for next year.

Next year, I'm going to study harder!

3 Work with a partner. Compare your resolutions.

Self-Assessment

Circle the correct alternative to complete the sentences.

1. **A:** Let's have a slumber party next weekend!
   B: Great! I**'ll bring**/**'m going to bring** some soda.
2. I **am not going**/**am going** to go to swim class today. It's very cold.
3. **Cars will fly**/**Will cars fly** in the year 3000?
4. **A:** Will houses be different in the future?
   B: Yes, they **will**/**are**.
5. What **will you do**/**are you going to do** next Sunday afternoon?
6. **A:** Would you like some juice?
   B: No, I think I**'ll have**/**'m going to have** some soda.
7. Look at the sky. It **is going to be**/**will be** a sunny day.
8. He **will have**/**is going to have** a barbecue with his family on Christmas Day.
9. **A:** Is she going to help you with your homework?
   B: Yes, she **is.**/**is going**.
10. **A:** Are you going to travel anywhere this weekend?
    B: No, **I'm not.**/**won't**.

What your score means…

8-10 Congratulations! You can understand and use the language learned in this unit.

5-7 Good job! How about looking back over pages 28 to 37? Then answer the questions again.

0-4 Oops… I'm sure you can do better! Let's try again! Go back to pages 28 to 37 and answer the questions. Ask your teacher for help.

Rewind 1

Units 1 - 2

1 Look at the pictures. What are these people thinking about? Match them with the future plans.

a. 

b. 

c. 

d. 

e. 

[ ] ...I'm going to hang out with my friends at the park.

[ ] ...I'm going to train for two or three hours a day.

[ ] ...I'm going to have a special birthday celebration.

[ ] ...I'm going to have dinner with my family.

[ ] ...I'm going to ride the Sugarloaf Mountain Cable Car.

2 These are Rafaela's plans for the weekend. Read the text and answer the questions.

Hmm... The weekend is coming... I love my weekends!
On Friday afternoon I'm going to hang out with my friends. We're going to watch Netflix series and listen to music at Veronica's house until 11 p.m. On Saturday morning I'm going to sleep until noon. I'm very tired. School tests are really hard this year. Then I'm going shopping with my mom. In the evening I'm going to stay home and have dinner with her. On Sunday I'm going to the movies with Jessica. We're going to see *Fantastic Beasts and Where to Find Them*. I'm very excited about that. Finally, on Sunday evening, I'm going to stay home, do my homework, and study for a test.

a. Who is Rafaela going to hang out with on Friday afternoon?

She's going to hang out with her friends.

b. What are Rafaela and her friends going to do at Veronica's house?

c. Why is she going to sleep until noon on Saturday morning?

d. What is she going to do when she gets up?

e. Is she going to do her homework and study for a test on Saturday evening?

3 Circle the correct option to complete the sentences.

a. Are you hungry? **I'll/I'm going to** make you something to eat.

b. I'm not free on Sunday evening. **I'll/I'm going to** do my homework and study for a test.

c. In a near future, people **will/are going to** probably stop reading printed books.

d. Look at this! They **will/are going to** build more houses in the area.

4 Read the poster and check (✓) the true statements.

a. Students have to say Please and Thank you. ☐

b. Students have to respect their teachers and classmates. ☐

c. Students don't have to be responsible. ☐

d. Students have to make mistakes. ☐

e. Students don't have to work hard. ☐

f. Students have to do their best. ☐

5 Read the poster again and complete the answer to the following question.

What do students have to do in relation to their belongings?

____________________ to themselves.

6 Go back to the poster. Which phrase encourages students to be brave?

____

7 Complete the sentences with *be going to*. Write affirmative and negative sentences.

a. There is nothing good on TV, so I ____________________.

b. His bike is broken, so he ____________________.

c. Our plants are dying, so Grandma ____________________.

d. It's very cold outside, so we ____________________.

unit

3 This place is more interesting!

IN THIS UNIT YOU WILL

- describe and compare cities and places
- talk about the location or position of one thing in relation to another
- learn words that are used when you cannot specify the exact amount of something
- learn some language used in restaurants

START UP

Let's plug in! Describe the two places shown in the pictures. Which one is similar to the place where you live? Which one is more interesting? Give reasons.

LOADING

1 **Alice has just come back from a vacation in Kyoto, Japan. Read and listen to a post about the city on her blog.**

22

Kyoto is a cosmopolitan city. Like any big city, it offers numerous opportunities to enjoy museums, galleries, botanical gardens, traditional temples, and markets. The city is full of cultural, artistic, and nature related events throughout the year.

Summers in Kyoto are hot and rainy. Winters are cold and it sometimes snows. Spring and fall are probably the best times to visit the city. During these months you can go hiking in the mountains, bike around the city, or walk in the gardens.

These are my favorite places in Kyoto:

a. **Nijo Castle -** In the past the castle was used as an imperial palace. Now it's open to public. Its buildings are very good examples of the architecture of Japan's feudal era.

b. **Nishiki Market -** This is a long shopping street market with more than one hundred stands and restaurants.

c. **Daigo-ji Temple -** This is well-known as the "Temple of Flowers". On the second Sunday of April, there is a feast to commemorate a famous cherry blossom.

d. **Kyoto Handicraft Center -** This is the best souvenir shop in Kyoto. You can find everything there – from dolls to jewelry.

e. **Flea markets -** Tourists love going to these! There are two very good flea markets in the city. Vendors sell clothes, tools, antiques, art, and plants.

Kyoto is the most bike-friendly city in Asia. If you enjoy cycling, rent a bike and explore the city!

2 **Read the post again and match the tourist attractions in Kyoto (a-e) with the pictures.**

UPLOADING

3 Match the adjectives with their meanings.

a. cosmopolitan	☐	relating to any form of art
b. numerous	☐	famous
c. cultural	☐	a place where people from many different countries and cultures live
d. artistic	☐	relating to the culture of a particular group, country, or society
e. feudal	☐	existing in large numbers
f. long	☐	covering a large distance
g. well-known	☐	relating to feudalism

Study this

Describing cities, places, and things

Kyoto is a **cosmopolitan** city.

It offers **numerous** opportunities to enjoy museums.

The city is full of **cultural** and **artistic** events.

Its buildings are very good examples of the architecture of Japan's **feudal** era.

This is a **long** shopping street market with more than one hundred stands and restaurants.

This is **well-known** as the "Temple of Flowers".

4 Complete the sentences with three adjectives from Activity 3.

a. It is a ____________ way to Tokyo from here.

b. Los Angeles is a cosmopolitan city with ____________ attractions for tourists.

c. I love to vist places with many ____________ activities like plays, concerts, and art exhibitions.

5 Listen to a description of Mumbai, an important city in India. Choose the correct words.

23

a. Mumbai is	✓	very populous.	☐	not very populous.
b. In July, the weather in the city is	☐	dry.	☐	rainy.
c. Its buildings are both	☐	modern and ancient.	☐	small and dirty.
d. Like any big city, Mumbai can be	☐	hot and cloudy.	☐	noisy and dirty.

DOWNLOADING

6 Describe your city.

Step 1: Use Alice's post in Activity 1 and the language in the Study this box to help you.

I live ____________.

My city is ____________

____________.

Step 2: Work with a partner. Compare your descriptions.

LOADING

1 (24) **Camila and Layla are working on a school project about big cities around the world. They are comparing information. Listen and read.**

New York City

Country	United States
State	New York
Area	1,200 km^2
Population	Over 8 million people
Temperature	9°C – 17°C
Languages spoken	800
Subway stations	472

São Paulo

Country	Brazil
State	São Paulo
Area	1,500 km^2
Population	Over 11 million people
Temperature	14°C – 24°C
Languages spoken	210
Subway stations	69

Camila: Look at this, Layla! São Paulo is bigger than New York City.

Layla: Yes, and it is more populous, too. There's a difference of three million people - that's a lot! What about the temperature?

Camila: Well, New York is not as warm as São Paulo. And I don't like the cold weather.

Layla: I don't like it either. But I'd love to visit New York one day. The number of subway stations is higher there. There are 472 stations in the city.

Camila: 472? So it is easier to get around then.

Layla: I guess so. On the other hand, it is more difficult to talk to people there.

Camila: Why?

Layla: People speak 800 languages!

Camila: Eight hundred? You could definitely find someone who speaks the same language as you.

2 **Look at the information again and write *NY* for New York and *SP* for São Paulo.**

a. There are over 11 million people living in this city. SP

b. The weather there is cold. ____

c. Layla would like to visit this city. ____

d. This city is bigger and more populous. ____

3 (25) **Listen again and repeat the dialogue.**

UPLOADING

Grammar feed

Comparatives

Superiority

One-syllable adjectives

New York is **colder than** São Paulo.

São Paulo is **bigger than** New York.

Two or more syllable adjectives

São Paulo is **more populous than** New York.

New York is **more attractive than** São Paulo.

Equality

New York is not **as warm as** São Paulo.

In my opinion, living in São Paulo is **as exciting as** living in New York.

Study this

B I G → BIGGER
↓ ↓ ↓ ↓
C V C → Double the last consonant

happy → ~~y~~ → happ**ier**

4 **Look at the information in the chart about how happy people are with their city. Then complete the sentences comparing the cities.**

	London	Lisbon	Madrid
People satisfied with their city	90-95%	75-90%	75-90%
People think it is easy to buy a house	10-19%	33-50%	19-33%
People happy with public transport	82%	61%	62-73%
People think administrative services are efficient	60-80%	40-60%	40-60%

a. People in London are *more satisfied* with their city *than* people in Lisbon.

b. People in Lisbon are ______ with their city ______ people in Madrid.

c. People in Lisbon think it is ______ to buy a house ______ people in London.

d. People in London are ______ people in Madrid.

e. People in London think administrative services are ______ in Lisbon.

f. People in Madrid think administrative services are ______ in Lisbon.

DOWNLOADING

5 **Work with a partner. Choose London, Lisbon, or Madrid. In your notebook, write four sentences comparing the city you live in to the city you have chosen.**

LOADING

1 **Listen and read these conversations.**

26

a.

b.

c.

d.

2 **Read the conversations again. Write T (true) or F (false).**

a. There is a bakery on Main Avenue. T F

b. The bus stop is across from the school. T F

c. The gym is next to the supermarket. T F

d. There is a bookstore in front of the bank. T F

3 **Listen again and repeat the dialogues.**

27

UPLOADING

Study this

Where is the kitten?

The kitten is **on** the keyboard.

The kitten is **under** the blanket.

The kitten is **next to** the vase.

The kitten is **behind** the vase.

The kitten is **between** the dogs.

The kitten is **in front of** the cushion.

The kitten is **across from** the park.

4 **Look at the pictures and write sentences that describe the position of the places.**

a.

park / school

The park is across from the school.

c.

bank / post office / restaurant

b.

drugstore / bookstore

d.

supermarket / newsstand

DOWNLOADING

5 **Think of a place in your neighborhood and write a sentence describing its location. Work with a partner. Tell him/her your sentence. Your partner draws what you describe.**

LOADING

1 **Sandy and James are having lunch in a restaurant. Listen and read their conversation.**

28

Waiter: Are you ready to order?
Sandy: Yes, we are.
Waiter: What would you like for your appetizer?
James: I'd like some French onion soup, please.
Sandy: And I'll have a tomato salad, please.
Waiter: And for your main?
James: I'd like a steak.
Waiter: OK. Would you like some French fries with that?
James: Yes, please.
Sandy: And I'd like roast chicken and rice, please.
Waiter: And to drink?
James: I'll have an orange juice.
Waiter: Sorry, sir. We don't have any juice.
James: I'll have mineral water then.
Sandy: And I'll have a soda.

Waiter: So, how was your meal?
Sandy: It was delicious, thanks.
Waiter: Would you like anything for dessert?
James: Is there any ice cream?
Waiter: No, sir. We have fruit salad and apple pie.
James: So… no dessert today. Thank you.

2 **Read the dialogue again and circle the food and drink they order.**

UPLOADING

Grammar feed

Some, Any, No

Interrogative, Affirmative and Negative sentences

Interrogative: Is there **any** ice cream?
Are there **any** sugar-free options?

Affirmative: I'd like **some** onion soup, please.
I'd like **some** French fries, please.

Negative: We don't have **any** juice.
I want **no** dessert today.

Offers and requests

Would you like **some** French fries? | Can I have **some** more water, please?

3 **Complete the sentences with *some*, *any*, or *no*.**

a. There is [no] coffee left. Can you get [some] coffee when you are out?

b. Can I have [ ] more tea, please?

c. I'd like a sandwich and [ ] mineral water.

d. There aren't [ ] bananas in the basket.

4 **Unscramble the words and write questions. Then check (✓) the ones that are requests.**

a. Can / have / I / please / some / water
Can I have some water, please? [ ]

b. Can / chicken / get / I / some / wings / you
[ ] [ ]

c. any / Do / have / salad / you
[ ] [ ]

DOWNLOADING

5 **You are in a restaurant. Complete the conversation.**

Waiter: Hello. Can I help you?
You: Yes, [ ].
Waiter: [ ] a starter?
You: Yes, I'd like [ ].
Waiter: And what [ ]?
You: [ ].
Waiter: [ ] like a drink?
You: Yes, [ ] a soda, please.

Your turn!

Work with a partner. Role-play the conversations you created.

iListen

1 Two teenagers are planning to go backpacking next January. Listen to their conversation and match the photos to the adjectives they use.

29

LEARNING STRATEGY

READING STRATEGY

Foz do Iguaçu, Brazil.

Machu Picchu, Peru.

ancient | beautiful | dangerous | fantastic | hot | rainy

iSpeak

2 What's your ideal city like? Write some information about it.

City: ______ Population: ______

Country: ______ Temperature: ______

State: ______ Languages spoken: ______

Area: ______ km^2 ______

Work with a partner. Compare your ideal city to his/hers.

My city is hotter in the summer than your city.

My city is more organized than your city.

iWrite

3 Write a blog post about the ideal city you created in Activity 2. Use the language you learned in this unit.

1 Have you ever met someone from another part of your country? What cultural differences did you notice? Exchange ideas with your classmates.

iThink

2 Read part of an article about barriers to intercultural communication. Can you explain the meaning of Ethnocentrism?

READING STRATEGY

BARRIERS TO **INTERCULTURAL COMMUNICATION**

by Karen Farnen • Updated September 29, 2017.

Even within the same culture, communication isn't always easy, so knowing the barriers to intercultural communication is the first step to overcome problems.

LANGUAGE DIFFERENCES

Language differences are an obvious barrier to intercultural communication. If you speak only English and a storekeeper speaks only Japanese, you won't be able to communicate verbally. Even if you've studied the language or an interpreter is available, dialects, different accents, and slang can cause problems. In addition, words don't necessarily translate from one language to another in a clean one-to-one correspondence. The same English word may have different meanings to people from different cultures.

BODY LANGUAGE

People sometimes take offense because of differences in body language across cultures. For example, a businessperson from Latin America might stand closer to a client than someone from North America would. This may make the North American feel crowded and want to back away. Also, Americans typically smile more than French people, and sometimes Americans think they aren't friendly.

NEGATIVE STEREOTYPES AND PREJUDICES

Stereotypes and prejudices about people from other cultures can cause communication problems and give offense. Ethnocentrism, or believing that your own culture is better than that of others, can lead to acting superior toward other groups and not treating them well.

3 Read the article again and mark the sentences T (true) or F (false).

a. Communication can be difficult between people from the same culture, too. T F

b. Different cultures can interpret a word in different ways. T F

c. American people don't smile as much as French people. T F

see word pop-up page 158

project

1 Play the comparisons game.

HOW TO PLAY THE GAME:

- Work with a partner. Place your counters on **START**.
- Flip a coin to move around the board. Heads = move 2 spaces. Tails = move 1 space.
- When you land on a space with an adjective, create a sentence comparing two places or things.
- If your sentence is correct, stay on the square. If you make a mistake, move one space back.
- The winner is the player who arrives at **FINISH** first.

2 Choose two pictures at a time and make sentences comparing them. Share your sentences with your classmates.

Self-Assessment

Circle the correct alternative to complete the sentences.

1. A big city is **interesting than/more interesting than** a small city.
2. Mumbai is **crowded than/more crowded than** Kyoto.
3. Like any other big city, Mexico City can be **noisy/noisier** and dirty.
4. Summer in Rio de Janeiro is **hotter/more hot** than in Sydney.
5. Victoria is 16 years old and Juliana is 19. Victoria **is not/is** as old as Juliana.
6. **A:** Would you like **any/some** French fries?
   B: Yes, please.
7. **A:** Is there **any/some** ice cream in the fridge?
   B: No, there is **no/any** ice cream left.
8. The bank is **between/across from** the school and the gym.

9. The newsstand is **on/in front of** the drugstore.

10. The bank is **between/next to** the restaurant.

What your score means...

8-10 Congratulations! You can understand and use the language learned in this unit.
5-7 Good job! How about looking back over pages 44 to 53? Then answer the questions again.
0-4 Oops... I'm sure you can do better! Let's try again! Go back to pages 44 to 53 and answer the questions. Ask your teacher for help.

unit

4 My city is the coolest!

» IN THIS UNIT YOU WILL

- express opinions using superlative adjectives
- learn words that describe people and places
- learn the difference between comparatives and superlatives
- agree and disagree with other people's opinions

START UP

Let's plug in! Can you identify the cities in the pictures? What do you know about each of them? In your opinion, which one is the best to live in? And which one is the coolest to visit on vacation? Explain.

LOADING

1 **Listen and read about some Brazilian cities. Then match the places with the texts.**

30

a. Brasília **b.** Curitiba **c.** Salvador **d.** São Paulo

[ ] This is an important cultural, political, and economical center in Latin America. The city preserves and cares for its green areas and it is considered one of the world's best examples of urban planning. With a population of over 3.2 million people, this is the largest city in Southern Brazil.

[ ] This city has one of the highest population growth rates in our country. Its international airport serves the metropolitan area with major domestic and international flights, and it is the third busiest Brazilian airport based on passengers and aircraft movements.

[ ] The city is home to several of the tallest skyscraper buildings in the country. It is also home to monuments, parks, and museums. The metropolitan region consists of 39 municipalities and it is known as the financial, economic, and cultural center of Brazil.

[ ] This city is noted for its cuisine, music, and architecture. The city is divided into two parts – Lower Town and Upper Town. An elevator connects the two parts of the city. A district in Upper Town is still home to many examples of Portuguese colonial architecture and historical monuments. Its metropolitan area forms the wealthiest area in Northeastern Brazil.

2 **Read the texts again and answer the questions.**

Which city...

a. represents the richest area in the northeast of the country? Salvador

b. is known as the financial, economic, and cultural center of Brazil? ____

c. has the third busiest airport in terms of passengers and aircraft movements? ____

d. is considered one of the world's best examples of urban planning? ____

3 **Which of the cities do you think is the most interesting?**

Grammar feed

Superlatives

One-syllable adjectives:

THE + ADJECTIVE + -EST

The city is home to several of **the tallest** skyscraper buildings.

Two or more syllable adjectives:

THE + MOST + ADJECTIVE

The most interesting city is Salvador.

UPLOADING

4 **The chart below gives some information about the Williams. Use the superlative of the adjectives in the box and write sentences about the members of the family.**

Name	Age	Height (cm)	Weight (kg)
Mr. Williams	43	180	78
Mrs. Williams	40	165	67
James	21	183	75
Janet	18	169	58

~~heavy~~	light	old
short	tall	young

a. Mr. Williams is the heaviest in the family.

b. ______

c. ______

d. ______

e. ______

f. ______

5 **Finish the sentences.**

a. A BMW is an expensive brand of car, but it is not the most expensive.

b. A rhinoceros is a dangerous animal, but ______.

c. Leonardo DiCaprio is a famous actor, but ______.

d. Kayaking is an amazing extreme sport, but ______.

DOWNLOADING

6 **Talk about some of your family members.**

Step 1: Write the name of a family member for each of the following categories.

- The youngest person: ______
- The friendliest person: ______
- The most responsible person: ______
- The most successful person: ______
- The funniest person: ______

Step 2: In pairs, ask questions about your partner's list of names.

LOADING

1 Stephanie and her friends are deciding where to eat. Listen and read.

31

Stephanie: So, where are we going to eat?
Josh: Let's go to Burger Queen. They have the best hamburgers in the city.
Stephanie: And the most expensive ones, too. Besides, I think the burgers at The Sixties are better than Burger Queen's.
Yuri: Well, I prefer the burgers at Big Burger.
Mitchel: Come on, guys! My mom makes the best burgers… and they're free!
Josh: Hey, that gives me an idea. Let's make our own hamburgers.
Yuri: No way. I'm too hungry. I want to eat right now.
Josh: Oh, OK. Let's go to Burger Queen then.
Stephanie: The Sixties.
Yuri: Big Burger.

2 Match the people from the dialogue in Activity 1 with their favorite places.

3 Listen again and repeat the dialogue.

32

Grammar feed

Comparatives vs. Superlatives

Comparing restaurants

Burger Queen	$$$
The Sixties	$$
Big Burger	$

The Sixties is **more expensive than** *Big Burger*, but *Burger Queen* is **the most expensive** restaurant.

Comparing people

Thais	23
Betty	19
Andrew	17

Betty is **younger than** Thais, but Andrew is **the youngest** in the family.

UPLOADING

4 **Use the words to write sentences.**

a. Spain / Italy / country in Europe (big)

Spain is bigger than Italy, but it isn't the biggest country in Europe.

b. Argentina / Uruguay / country in South America (large)

____

c. The math teacher / the literature teacher / teacher at school (experienced)

____

d. A tiger / a bear / animal in the world (dangerous)

____

5 **Compare the items. Complete the sentences with your opinion.**

a.

History

Math

English

I think __________ is harder than __________ , but __________ is the hardest subject.

b.

Scarlett Johansson

Jennifer Lawrence

Emma Watson

In my opinion, __________ is more famous than __________ , but __________ is the most famous actress.

c.

Wonder Woman

Spiderman

Logan

To me, __________ is more exciting than __________ , but __________ is the most exciting super hero.

DOWNLOADING

6 **Work with a partner. Share your opinion about the items in Activity 5.**

I think history is more difficult than math, but English is the most difficult subject.

In my opinion, math is the most difficult subject.

LOADING

1 **Listen and read these conversations. Which superlative adjective isn't irregular?**

33

a.

b.

c.

d.

2 **Read the conversations again. Then circle the correct information.**

a. To Maria, **the worst/the best** place in the country is Toledo.

b. In Adam's opinion, the Mexican restaurant is **better/worse** than the Indian restaurant.

c. The couple can't go any **further/furthest** because the road is blocked.

3 **Listen again and repeat the dialogues.**

34

Study this

Irregular Comparative and Superlative forms

		Comparative		Superlative
bad	–	worse than	–	the worst
far	–	further / farther than	–	the furthest / farthest
good	–	better than	–	the best

Study this

		Comparative		Superlative
funny	–	funn**ier** than	–	the funn**iest**
ugly	–	ugl**ier** than	–	the ugl**iest**
heavy	–	heav**ier** than	–	the heav**iest**

UPLOADING

4 **Complete with irregular comparative adjectives.**

a. I can't keep walking. I'm very tired. Is the bus stop much ______?

b. I don't like traveling by train, except when I am in France. The trains there are ______.

c. **A:** How's your fever?

B: It's getting ______. I'm going to see a doctor.

5 **Complete the sentences. Use the comparative or the superlative form of the adjectives in parentheses.**

a. My brother's room is tidier than mine. (tidy)

b. Australia is ______ England. (big)

c. Who is ______ person in your family? (funny)

d. Chinese is ______ language to learn. (difficult)

e. I think cats are ______ dogs. (intelligent)

f. Lara has ______ grades in the class. (good)

g. This is ______ ice cream in the ice cream parlor. (bad)

6 **Match the columns to make sentences.**

a. Brian is	[ ] the biggest state	[ ] in the band.
b. My grandfather is	[ ] the longest river	[ ] in my family.
c. London is	[ ] the best musician	[a] in his team.
d. Alaska is	[a] the slowest runner	[ ] in Africa.
e. The guitar player is	[ ] the biggest city	[ ] in Britain.
f. The Nile is	[ ] the oldest person	[ ] in the U.S.A.

DOWNLOADING

7 **Write an ending for each sentence. Use comparatives or superlatives. In groups of three, read your sentences and choose the best ones.**

a. My mother is very careful with money. She is ______.

b. I'm hungry, but ______.

c. We're very excited about the trip. We are ______.

LOADING

1 Josh, Stephanie, Yuri, and Mitchel are having lunch at Burger Queen. Listen and read.

35

Josh: So guys, tell me what you think about these hamburgers.

Stephanie: You're right, Josh! They're delicious.

Yuri: I'm with you, Josh. They are the best burgers in the city, but they are very expensive.

Josh: Yes, they are the most expensive burgers in the city.

Mitchel: Well, I don't think these burgers are better than my mom's.

Josh: All right, Mitchel. We'll have your mom's hamburgers next time.

Mitchel: Deal! Let's meet next Friday night at my house.

Stephanie: Sorry, Friday is family day at my place. I'll stay at home. I like spending time with my family. We usually play games and order pizza.

Josh: I agree with you. Spending time with our family is very important and fun, too.

2 Read the dialogue again and answer.

a. Does Stephanie like the hamburgers? *Yes, she does.*

b. Does Yuri think they are the best burgers? ______

c. Does Mitchel say those burgers are better than his mom's? ______

d. Is Stephanie going to have dinner at Mitchel's house next Friday? ______

e. Does Josh agree with Stephanie? ______

f. Does Stephanie usually have hamburgers on Friday night? ______

3 Listen again and repeat the dialogue.

36

Study this

Giving opinions, agreeing, and disagreeing

Giving opinions	Agreeing	Disagreeing
I believe that…	I agree with you.	I don't agree with you.
(Personally), I think…	I'm with you.	I don't think...
In my opinion…	I think so.	Sorry, I have to say "No".
	That's so true.	Yes, but don't you think…?
	You're right.	

UPLOADING

4 **Match the sentences and form short dialogues.**

a. I think traveling by train is fantastic.

b. I believe that our city is a great place for tourists.

c. Personally, I think this movie is better than the one we watched last week.

d. I think living in the country is better than living in the city.

[ ] I agree with you. There is plenty for visitors to do here.

[ ] I don't agree with you. There is so much more we can do in the city!

[ ] I don't think so. This movie is so boring!

[ ] You can't be serious. It's so tiring!

5 **Order the sentences (1-6) and form dialogues.**

A.

[ ] How do you feel about iLearn Rock Band?

[ ] It is amazing! Oh... you have lots of rock DVDs here!

[ ] I think so, too. I'd say they are the best rock band ever.

[ ] They're great!

[1] What do you think of my new bedroom?

[ ] Yeah, I have a few. Rock is my favorite kind of music.

B.

[ ] It's good, but my mom's cake is better.

[ ] Let me see if I can find it...

[ ] So give me the recipe.

[ ] Tell me what you think about my chocolate cake.

[ ] Sorry, but her chocolate topping is delicious!

[ ] You can't be serious!

DOWNLOADING

6 **Write your opinion about a band or singer, a movie or TV series, and a book. Use the expressions from the box on page 66.**

Band/singer: ____________________

Movie/series: ____________________

Book: ____________________

Your turn!

Talk to your classmate and share your opinion on the items you listed in Activity 6.

iSkills

iSpeak

1 **Work with a partner. Use the cues in the chart to ask him/her questions. Write his/her answers in the chart. Don't forget to use the superlative forms of the adjectives.**

Question cues	Classmate's answers
a. Who / amazing / actress in Brazil?	
b. Who / good / soccer player in the world?	
c. What / difficult / school subject?	
d. What / cool / brand of sneakers?	

Mariana, who is the best actress in Brazil?

Hmm... I think it's Bruna Marquezine.

iWrite

2 **Use your partner's answers from Activity 1 to write a paragraph about his/her opinions.**

In Mariana's opinion, the best actress in Brazil is Bruna Marquezine.

iListen

3 **Listen to the conversations and circle the correct alternatives.**

LEARNING STRATEGY

37

a.

b.

c.

1 Match the animals with the pictures. Do you know any interesting facts about them?

a. dog **b.** lioness **c.** gorilla **d.** lion **e.** ostrich **f.** pig **g.** spider **h.** Chinese water deer

2 Read some facts about the animals in Activity 1. Then check (✓) the sentence that is similar in meaning to the one presented.

Interesting and surprising facts about animals

If you want to know some cool and surprising facts about animals, here are some of the best ones!

- Gorillas can get human colds and other sicknesses.
- A baby Chinese water deer is so tiny it can almost fit in your hand.
- Ostriches can run faster than horses, and male ostriches can make sounds like lions.
- A lion living in wild areas usually makes no more than twenty kills a year.
- Female lions do most of the hunting, which is about ninety percent.
- Nearly half of the world's pigs are raised by farmers in China.
- Dogs generally see better than humans, but they can't see as many colors.
- On average, there are 50,000 spiders per acre in green areas.

see word pop-up page 162

A lion living in wild areas usually makes no more than twenty kills a year.

☐ The minimum number of kills a lion in the wild usually makes in one year is twenty.

☐ The maximum number of kills a lion in the wild usually makes in one year is twenty.

READING STRATEGY

3 Answer the questions. Which animal…

a. runs faster than horses? Ostriches

b. has better eyesight than humans? ______

c. is very numerous in green areas? ______

d. can catch human diseases? ______

1 Work with a partner. Can you solve these brain teasers?

a. I am bigger and also smaller than you. At times, I lead and sometimes I follow, too. I weigh nothing. What am I? ____________

b. What has four legs, but can't walk? ____________

c. What can you find in the middle of water? ____________

2 Complete the sentences with the superlative forms of the adjectives in the box. Then find the superlatives in the word search.

big
long
~~old~~
small
tall

A	R	R	Y	V	O	L	K	R	H	E	N	D	V	T	B	S	P	X	N
G	S	T	S	N	D	T	B	X	C	G	R	U	S	X	P	G	O	D	X
B	C	T	M	X	Q	N	C	Z	W	X	Y	E	W	R	R	L	H	Q	Q
B	O	U	A	J	M	G	U	B	T	C	L	L	W	Y	Y	O	W	G	Y
T	L	P	L	T	W	A	Z	O	X	L	T	A	L	R	N	N	E	J	S
C	D	X	L	V	N	A	O	T	A	I	N	U	P	S	C	G	A	P	Z
K	E	H	E	B	P	R	B	T	O	H	V	T	A	F	G	E	Z	F	U
W	S	L	S	Z	E	U	T	O	F	I	I	S	D	H	H	S	A	J	J
T	T	B	T	X	E	J	E	Y	V	B	I	G	G	E	S	T	S	E	S

Amazing Animal World Records

a. The giraffe is the tallest land animal. It can reach over 5 meters.

b. The ____________ snake is the Asian reticulated python. It can measure over 9 meters.

c. The Kitti's hog-nosed bat is the ____________ mammal. It measures about 3 centimeters.

d. The ____________ land predator is the polar bear. It even eats humans!

e. The ____________ cat ever was called Creme Puff. She was 38 years old when she died in 2005.

3 Work with a partner. Can you answer these questions?

a.

Why aren't bats considered birds?

____

b.

Are elephants really afraid of mice?

____

Self-Assessment

Circle the correct alternative to complete the sentences.

1. Salvador represents **the richest/richer** area in the northeast of the country.
2. Curitiba is **the most interesting/more interesting** city in Brazil.
3. India is an amazing country, but it is not **the more amazing/the most amazing** country in the world.
4. Argentina is **larger than/more large** than Uruguay, but it is not the largest country in South America.
5. We can't go **furthest/further** because the avenue is blocked.
6. This is **the worst/the worse** ice cream they produce in this ice cream parlor.
7. The black dress is **the most beautiful/the more beautiful** you have.
8. **A:** I think traveling by bus is fantastic.
   B: I **don't agree/agree** with you. Planes are safer and faster than buses.
9. **A:** These shoes are too old to wear to a party. Don't you think so?
   B: I agree with you./I don't think so. You should buy new ones.
10. **A:** I believe Fernanda Lima is the most beautiful woman on TV.
    B: I don't too./I do too. She's great.

What your score means...

8-10 Congratulations! You can understand and use the language learned in this unit.
5-7 Good job! How about looking back over pages 58 to 67? Then answer the questions again.
0-4 Oops... I'm sure you can do better! Let's try again! Go back to pages 58 to 67 and answer the questions. Ask your teacher for help.

1 Look at the pictures and read the information given. Compare the items using the adjectives from the box.

cold ~~old~~ populous

a. 

Siam Park in Spain
Opened to the public in 2008

Typhoon Lagoon in the United States
Opened to the public in 1989

Typhoon Lagoon in the United States is older than Siam Park in Spain.

b. 

Shanghai, China
Population: 24,256,800

Beijing, China
Population: 21,516,000

____

c. 

Dome Fuji, Antarctica
Temperature: -93.2 ºC
(in August 2010)

Vostok Research Station, Antarctica
Temperature: -89.2 ºC
(in July 1983)

____

2 Read these hotel reviews and decide if the sentences are T (true) or F (false).

"In a superb downtown location with views of Burj Khalifa, this three-star hotel sets a new standard for inexpensive hotels in Dubai. As fashionable as it is homely, Rove Downtown features quirky décor, an outdoor pool, an excellent restaurant, and relaxed service. In short, it's brilliant."

"One&Only The Palm is one of Dubai's most secluded and attractive beachside resorts, offering three restaurants by Michelin-starred French chef Yannick Alléno, indulgent spa treatments from the UAE's only Guerlain Spa, and a spectacular pool."

"The family-friendly Four Seasons Resort Dubai is home to Mercury, one of Dubai's – if not the world's – coolest rooftop bars. When you're not admiring the views, take a walk in the colorful gardens or enjoy the private beach."

a. One of the most attractive spa resorts in Dubai is One&Only The Palm. T F

b. The number of restaurants in Rove Downtown Dubai is higher than in One&Only The Palm. T F

3 Read the sentences and find the places.

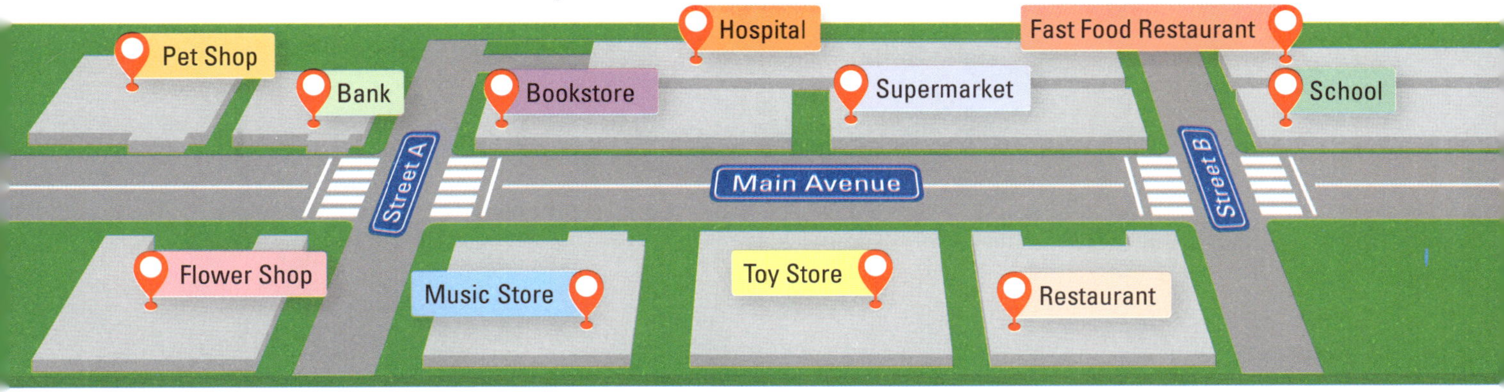

a. It's across from the restaurant.

Supermarket

b. It's between the music store and the restaurant.

c. It's next to the pet shop.

d. It's across from the bank.

4 Complete these conversations. Use *some*, *any*, or *no*.

a. **A:** Is there ______ coffee?

B: No, but I think there is ______ tea. Would you like ______ ?

A: Yes, please.

B: Would you like a cookie, too?

A: No, thanks.

b. **A:** I'm really hungry. Let's eat.

B: OK. I have ______ chicken in the refrigerator. Would you like ______ ?

A: Yes, please. Are there ______ vegetables?

B: There are ______ vegetables. I'm sorry.

A: So let's prepare ______ rice to have with the chicken.

5 Respond to these situations.

a. One of your classmates says: "Let's have something to eat after class."

You can't go because you have a doctor's appointment.

You say: ______

b. Your cousin is at your house and says: "I really like this game. Let's play it!"

You don't like the game very much.

You say: ______

c. Your best friend says: "I love surfing on weekends."

Surfing is your favorite free-time activity.

You say: ______

unit 5

Oldies but goodies.

IN THIS UNIT YOU WILL

- refer to the existence of something or someone in the past
- talk about actions that started and finished at a specific time in the past
- learn how to use the Simple Past with regular verbs

START UP

Let's plug in! What electronic gadgets can you see in the picture? Are they new? How different are they from the ones we use today? Do you think old electronic gadgets were as good as the ones we have now? Give reasons.

LOADING

1 **Steve Jobs and Mark Zuckerberg are two of the most influential people in the history of technology. Listen and read their biographies.** LEARNING STRATEGY

38

Steven Jobs was born on February 24th, 1955, in San Francisco, California. His adoptive parents were Paul and Clara Jobs. Paul was a machinist. Steve remembered his father as having special abilities with his hands.

When Steve was 20 years old, he was a member of the Homebrew Computer Club. There he was friends with a young man named Steve Wozniak. Steve J. and Steve W. were the creators of Apple Computer Company.

Steve's most important creations were Apple II in 1977, the Macintosh in 1984, the iPod in 2001, and the iPhone in 2007.

He died when he was 56 years old.

Mark Zuckerberg was born on May 14th, 1984, in White Plains, New York. His parents were Edward and Karen. Edward was a dentist and Karen was a psychiatrist.

When he was in middle school, he learned "Atari Basic Programming" from his father. He was tutored by David Newman, a software programmer, so Mark learned everything about programming from him.

Mark was a student at Harvard University. His most important creations were the website Thefacebook.com in 2004, Facebook Platform in 2007, and Internet.org in 2013.

Mark has a net worth of 36 billion dollars.

2 **Complete the chart with information from the biographies.**

	Steve Jobs	Mark Zuckerberg
Date of birth		
Place of birth		
Important creations	1977 - Apple II	

Grammar feed

Past of *To Be*

Yes/No Questions

Were you born in Curitiba?

Yes, I **was**.

No, I **wasn't**.

Was Steve Jobs very intelligent?

Yes, he **was**.

But he **wasn't** a very good student.

Question Words

When were you born?

I **was** born in December.

I **wasn't** born in May. I **was** born in April.

Where was Mark Zuckerberg born?

He **was** born in San Francisco, California.

Study this

wasn't = was + not

weren't = were + not

UPLOADING

3 **Read these short biographies. Fill in the blanks with the correct past form of *to be*.**

a. Rosa Parks was a civil rights activist. She ______ born on February 4th, 1913 in the United States. She ______ famous for fighting for racial equality when African Americans ______ discriminated against in the United States.

b. Zumbi ______ a famous leader of Quilombo dos Palmares. He ______ a slave when he ______ a child. He ______ born in 1655, and he ______ 40 years old at the time of his death, on November 20th, 1695.

4 **Answer these questions.**

a.

1960

Was Ayrton Senna a car racer?

Yes, he was.

When was he born?

He was born in 1960.

b.

London

Was David Bowie American?

______

Where was he from?

______

c.

Spain

Were Picasso and Dali from France?

______

Where were they from?

______

d.

1954

Was Nina Simone a pianist and singer?

______

When was she born?

______

DOWNLOADING

5 **Work with a partner. Choose two famous people and find out more about them.**

A: When were you born?
B: I was born on August 3rd, 2004.
A: Where were you born?
B: I was born in São Paulo.

Study this

1st	first	6th	sixth	20th	twentieth
2nd	second	7th	seventh	24th	twenty-fourth
3rd	third	8th	eighth	30th	thirtieth
4th	fourth	9th	ninth		
5th	fifth				

LOADING

1 Listen and read about some technological breakthroughs from the 20th century and their most modern versions.

39

SOMETIME IN THE 20TH CENTURY

NOWADAYS

In the late 1920s, there were cathode ray tube televisions.

Nowadays, there are flat screen televisions.

In 1950, there were big and heavy computers.

Nowadays, there are very fast personal computers.

In 1979, there were audio cassette players.

Nowadays, there are music apps for mobile devices.

In 1972, there was only one video game console.

Nowadays, there are many different kinds of video game consoles.

There were cell phones in 1983.

Nowadays, there are smartphones.

Study this

Present		Past
There is	→	There was
There are	→	There were

Grammar feed

Past of *There is/There are*

***Yes/No* Questions**

Were there personal computers in 1950?
Yes, **there were**. **There was** a computer called Simon.

Were there cell phones in 1950?
No, **there weren't**.

UPLOADING

2 **Complete the questions with *Was there* or *Were there*. Then answer the questions.**

a. Were there payphones in 1920? Yes, there were.
b. ________ computers at schools in 1980? No, ________.
c. ________ a park in the neighborhood in 1980? Yes, ________.
d. ________ Internet in homes in 1990? No, ________.
e. ________ air pollution in 1960? Yes, ________.
f. ________ astronauts in 1940? No, ________.
g. ________ hospitals in 1910? Yes, ________.
h. ________ radio in 1940? Yes, ________.

3 **Use the prompts to create affirmative or negative sentences. Pay attention to the signs in parentheses.**

a. There / a beautiful lake here / in 1975 (✓)
There was a beautiful lake here in 1975.

b. There / many cars on the streets there / in 1910 (**X**)
There weren't

c. There / a huge tree / here when I was a kid (✓)
____

d. There / two bakeries there / in 1999 (**X**)
____

Study this

here →
there →

DOWNLOADING

4 **Work with a partner. Take turns asking and answering questions about inventions in 1920, 1960, and 2012. Use the information in the chart.**

Were there airplanes in 1920?

Yes, there were.

	In 1920	In 1960	In 2012
airplanes	✓	✓	✓
antibiotics		✓	✓
microwave ovens		✓	✓
televisions		✓	✓
Internet			✓
air conditioning	✓	✓	✓

LOADING

1 Listen and read Katherine's blog entry.

40

A Boring Saturday

Last Saturday wasn't very special. First, I helped my mom around the house. My room was a mess! So I cleaned my room (1). Next, I washed the dishes (2). After that, I walked Cappuccino, our dog (3). My brothers stayed home because it was so hot (but they didn't clean their bedroom!).

After lunch, I studied for my math test (4) (I hope I do well on the test!). Then I played *The Legend of Zelda* (5), my favorite video game, and chatted with Lauren online (6) for hours.

In the evening, I was really tired… and bored! I didn't watch TV and I didn't listen to music. Finally, I turned off the lights (7) at 10 o'clock and… off to sleep. What a boring day!

2 Match the numbered activities in Katherine's blog entry to the pictures.

Grammar feed

Simple Past: Regular Verbs

Affirmative	I **cleaned** my room.
	She **chatted** with Lauren online.
	They **stayed** home.
Negative	I **didn't watch** TV.
	She **didn't listen** to music.
	They **didn't clean** their bedroom.

Study this

didn't = did + not

didn't watch

~~didn't watched~~

chat → chat**ted**

study → stud**ied**

Study this

Past time expressions

yesterday

last Saturday / Monday / week

UPLOADING

3 **Look at Katherine's entry in Activity 1. Write the past forms of the verbs.**

a. to chat → chatted

b. to clean → ______

c. to help → ______

d. to play → ______

e. to stay → ______

f. to study → ______

g. to turn → ______

h. to walk → ______

i. to wash → ______

LEARNING STRATEGY

4 **Rewrite the sentences in the Simple Past.**

a. My cousins don't walk their dog every day.

My cousins didn't walk their dog yesterday.

b. She studies English on Sundays.

______ last Sunday.

c. He doesn't watch movies on TV on Mondays.

______ last Monday.

d. We help our classmates on Fridays.

______ last Friday.

DOWNLOADING

5 **Brian did many things on Saturday. Look at the pictures and complete his blog entry. Use the Simple Past.**

a.

b.

c.

d.

A great Saturday!

Saturday was a great day! In the morning, my mom said I didn't need to clean my bedroom! Yay! So I decided to have some fun.

First, I played soccer with my friends. Then, I ______ our dog. He was really happy. After lunch, I ______ my favorite action movie again. Finally, I ______ with Eric online and ______ to music.

Your turn!

Work with a partner. Did you do the same things as Brian did?

A: I played soccer.

B: I didn't play soccer, but I watched a movie.

LOADING

1 **Mike is asking George about his last vacation. Listen and read.**

41

Mike: So, did you travel during your vacation?
George: Yes, I did. I traveled to Fortaleza.
Mike: That's great! Did you go with your family?
George: Yes, I did. It was an amazing trip. We did many things there.
Mike: Did you visit the water park?
George: Of course we did! We spent two days there. I loved it. What about you? Did you go anywhere?
Mike: No, I didn't, but I had a good time, too. I played soccer with my friends. I also watched a lot of movies.

2 **Read the dialogue again. Then complete the sentences.**

a. George visited Fortaleza on his vacation.
b. Mike ________ soccer with his friends and ________ a lot of movies.
c. George ________ the water park.

3 **Listen again and repeat the dialogue.**

42

4 **Complete the chart with words from the box to form activities you can do when you are on vacation.**

~~a movie~~ Asian food favorite songs for the homeless with friends the guitar my grandparents

watch	TV a movie	**play**	video games
travel	with my family	**cook**	
visit	Fortaleza	**listen to**	some music

Grammar feed

Simple Past: *Yes/No* Questions

	Did you **travel** anywhere on your vacation?	**Did** your sister **like** the movie?
Affirmative	Yes, I **did**.	Yes, she **did**.
Negative	No, I **didn't**.	No, she **didn't**.

Study this

Did you visit Fortaleza?
~~Yes, I visited.~~
Yes, I did.

UPLOADING

5 Match the questions with the answers.

a.	Did Liz play volleyball on Saturday?	☐	No, they didn't. Their grandparents visited them.
b.	Did they visit their grandparents on their vacation?	☐	No, I didn't. I cooked Asian food.
c.	Did you listen to Taylor Swift's latest song yesterday?	☐	Yes, I did. And I loved it!
d.	Did you cook Italian food on Sunday?	☐	Yes, she did. She had a great time!

6 Look at the pictures below and the chart in Activity 4. Then complete the questions.

a.

A: Did you watch a movie yesterday?

B: Yes, I did. And the movie was great!

b.

A: ________ you ________ on your vacation?

B: Yes, I did. We traveled to Australia for ten days.

c.

A: ________ Bruno ________ the old ________?

B: Yes, he did. And he listened to new songs on his phone, too.

d.

A: ________ video games?

B: Yes, they did. They played all day long.

DOWNLOADING

7 Work with a partner. Take turns asking and answering about your last vacation.

A: Did you travel on your vacation?

B: Yes, I did. OR No, I didn't.

Your turn!

Report your answers to your classmates.

iRead

1 **Read the synopsis of Michael Jackson's biography. Then underline three regular verbs in the Simple Past.**

MICHAEL JACKSON

Michael Jackson had a very successful career with the Jackson 5 and on his own. In 1982, he released 'Thriller,' which became the best-selling album ever.

Synopsis

Michael Joseph Jackson, called the "King of Pop," was a famous American singer, songwriter, and dancer. Born on August 29, 1958, he became the lead singer of the Jackson 5, a popular Motown group, when he was a child. Later, he had a hugely successful solo career with No. 1 hits from albums like Off the Wall, Thriller, and Bad. He passed away on June 25, 2009.

2 **These sentences about Michael Jackson contain incorrect information. In pairs, correct them.**

a. This text is an album review.

This text is a biography.

b. Michael Jackson was British.

c. He was born in June 1958.

d. He was the lead singer of Jackson 10.

e. He released his best-selling album in 1988.

f. He died in 2008.

iListen

3 (43) **Listen to some information about two famous people and number the pictures.**

Salvador Dali
1904-1989

Jane Austen
1775-1817

1 You are going to read a brief introduction to the history of the Web. Scan the text and circle the name of the technology Sir Tim Berners-Lee used to create it.

READING STRATEGY

HISTORY OF THE WEB

Sir Tim Berners-Lee invented the World Wide Web in 1989.

Sir Tim Berners-Lee is a computer scientist from Britain. He was born in London, and his parents were also computer scientists who worked on one of the first computers.

As a child, Sir Tim Berners-Lee was fascinated by trains and had a model railway in his bedroom. He remembers making electronic devices to control the trains, which eventually led to a greater interest in electronics than in trains. Later, while in college, he built a computer using an old television set.

After finishing his studies at Oxford University, Berners-Lee worked as a software engineer at CERN, a major particle physics lab near Geneva, Switzerland. He observed that scientists from around the globe, who came to use the lab's accelerators, were struggling to share information.

Tim explains that back then, information was stored on different computers and accessing it required logging into each one separately. Additionally, each computer often had its own unique program that they needed to learn. As a result, it was often simpler to just ask people directly when they were taking a coffee break.

Tim believed he had a solution to this problem; one that could be widely useful. With millions of computers being linked through the rapidly growing Internet, Berners-Lee realized that they could share information by exploiting an emerging technology called hypertext.

In March 1989, Tim outlined his idea for what would later become the web in a document titled "Information Management: a Proposal." Surprisingly, his initial proposal wasn't immediately accepted. His boss, Mike Sendall, even wrote "Vague but exciting" on the cover. Although the Web was never an official CERN project, Mike allowed Tim to start working on it in September 1990. Tim began his work using a NeXT computer, an early product from Steve Jobs.

By October 1990, Tim had developed the three core technologies that still form the basis of today's web: HTML, URL, and HTTP.

2 Find the words below in the text. Then match each word with its meaning.

see word pop-up page 166

project

a. accelerator	☐	have or use something with other people
b. share	☐	a machine used to make small pieces of matter move faster
c. exploiting	☐	trying to get as much as you can out of a situation, sometimes unfairly

rePlay

1 The pictures below show a famous avenue in the capital of São Paulo in the 1900's and in the 2000's. Compare them pointing out the differences and similarities. Then write sentences that describe the picture on the left. Use *there was*, *there were*, *there wasn't*, or *there weren't*.

Paulista Avenue inauguration, 1891. São Paulo.

Aerial view of Paulista Avenue, 2017. São Paulo.

2 Let's play Memory Game! Work in groups of 3. You have one minute to study the chart below. Close your books. In your notebook, list the verbs from the chart in the Simple Past.

stay, clean, study, experience, visit, perform, remember, chat, decide, learn, wash, move, listen, move, travel, help, cook, play, die, walk, turn, develop

Self-Assessment

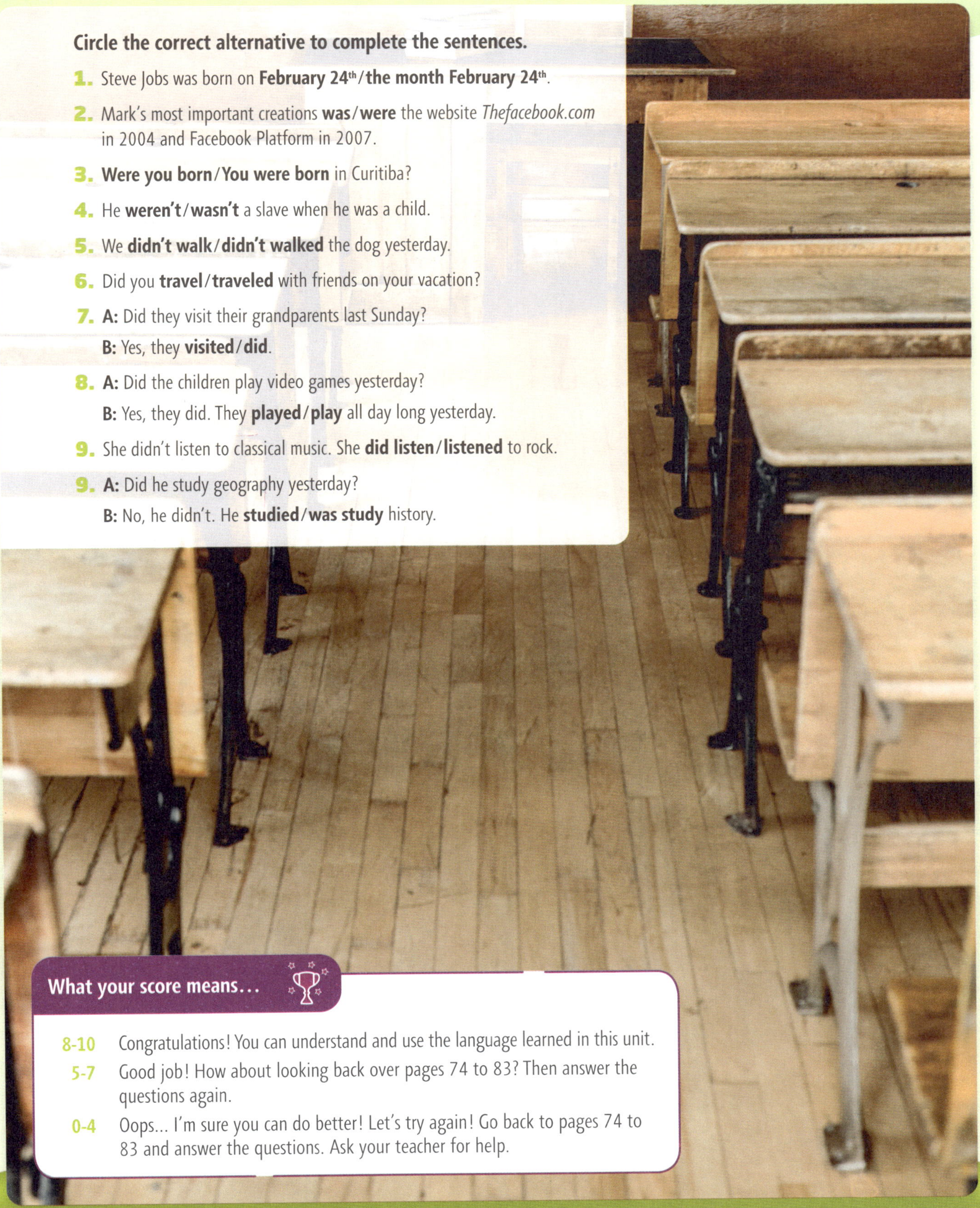

Circle the correct alternative to complete the sentences.

1. Steve Jobs was born on **February 24th/the month February 24th**.
2. Mark's most important creations **was/were** the website *Thefacebook.com* in 2004 and Facebook Platform in 2007.
3. **Were you born/You were born** in Curitiba?
4. He **weren't/wasn't** a slave when he was a child.
5. We **didn't walk/didn't walked** the dog yesterday.
6. Did you **travel/traveled** with friends on your vacation?
7. **A:** Did they visit their grandparents last Sunday?
   B: Yes, they **visited/did**.
8. **A:** Did the children play video games yesterday?
   B: Yes, they did. They **played/play** all day long yesterday.
9. She didn't listen to classical music. She **did listen/listened** to rock.
9. **A:** Did he study geography yesterday?
   B: No, he didn't. He **studied/was study** history.

What your score means...

8-10 Congratulations! You can understand and use the language learned in this unit.
5-7 Good job! How about looking back over pages 74 to 83? Then answer the questions again.
0-4 Oops... I'm sure you can do better! Let's try again! Go back to pages 74 to 83 and answer the questions. Ask your teacher for help.

unit 6 Did you have a good weekend?

IN THIS UNIT YOU WILL

- talk about past activities
- learn some linking words for sequencing facts
- make arrangements

START UP

Let's plug in! Did you do anything special last weekend? What did you do? Was it fun?

LOADING

1 **Look at what Thiago usually does on weekends and what he did last Saturday. Read and listen.** LEARNING STRATEGY

44

Thiago usually **gets up** at 6:30.

He **got up** at 11 o'clock last Saturday.

He **doesn't** usually **hang out** with his friends.

He **hung out** with his friends.

He **goes** to school.

He **didn't go** to school last Saturday. He **went** to the movie theater.

He always **does** his homework.

He **didn't do** his homework. He **did** crossword puzzles.

He usually **has** dinner at home.

He **had** dinner at a hamburger place.

He never **eats** pizza.

He **ate** a delicious pizza.

Grammar feed

Simple Past: Irregular Verbs

Affirmative and Negative Sentences

Affirmative	Thiago **got up** late. He **hung out** with his friends.	**Negative**	He **didn't go** to school. He **didn't do** his homework.

2 Read Thiago's Saturday activities again and check (✓) the correct statement(s).

a. He didn't get up at 6:30. He got up at 11 o'clock. ☐

b. He did his homework and crossword puzzles. ☐

c. He didn't eat pizza. ☐

3 Look at what these people did last Saturday. Complete the sentences using the past form of the verbs from the box. Refer to the list of irregular verbs on pages 144 and 145.

to go	~~to read~~	to ride	to sleep

a.

Sue didn't read a magazine. She read a book.

b.

Bruno ________ his bike on the street. He ________ his bike in the park.

c.

Maria ________ at Kayla's house. She ________ at Laura's house.

d.

Cathy ________ to her grandma's house. She ________ to the shopping mall.

DOWNLOADING

4 You're texting your friend to tell him/her about last weekend. Write four sentences about it. Choose verbs from the irregular verbs list on pages 144 and 145.

____

____

____

____

Your turn!

Work with a partner. Compare your sentences.

LOADING

1 **Reporters from the *iLearn Middle School Newsletter* interviewed some students to find out what they did last weekend. Read the graphs and check their answers.**

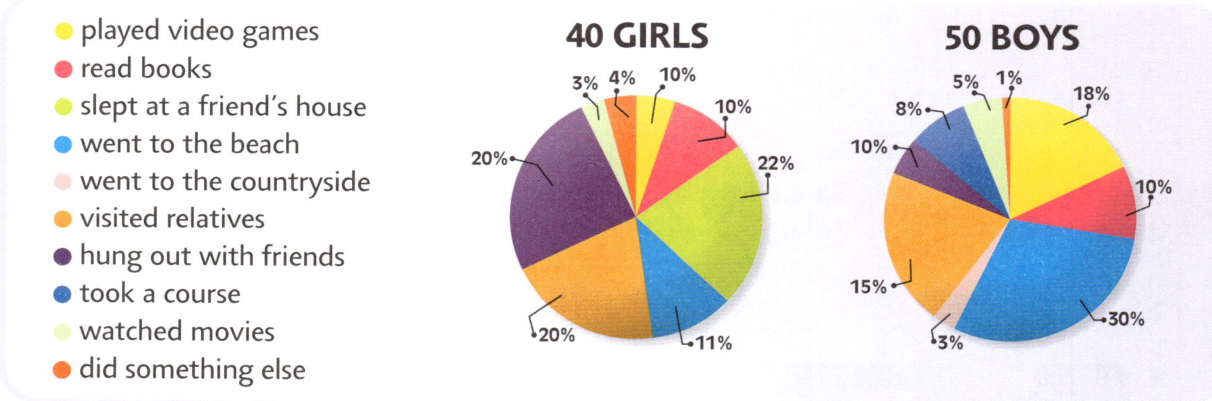

2 **Read the graphs again and answer the questions. Write numbers only.**

How many

a. ...students did the reporters interview? ______

b. ...girls and boys read books? ______

c. ...boys went to the beach? ______

d. ...girls visited relatives? ______

3 **Answer the questions below. Refer to the irregular verbs list on pages 144 and 145, if necessary.**

GIRLS

a. What didn't they do? They didn't go to the countryside and ______.

b. What was the most popular activity? ______ was the most popular activity.

c. What was the least popular activity? ______ was the least popular activity.

BOYS

d. What didn't the boys do? ______.

e. What was the most popular activity? ______ was the most popular activity.

f. What was the least popular activity? ______.

Grammar feed

Simple Past: Irregular Verbs

Interrogative Sentences

Did the girls **read** books?
Yes, they **did**.

Did the boys **sleep** at a friend's house?
No, they **didn't**.

Study this

~~Did you went to school yesterday?~~
Did you go to school yesterday?

UPLOADING

4 **Larissa is telling Ian about her last weekend. Listen and read.**

45

Ian: Hi, Larissa! How was your weekend?
Larissa: Hi, Ian. It was a lot of fun.
Ian: Really? What did you do?
Larissa: I went to the mall with my mom on Saturday morning. Then I hung out with some friends in the afternoon. After that I went to a friend's house and slept there.
Ian: That's great!
Larissa: Yes, I had a very good time. What about you? Where did you go?
Ian: Well, I didn't go anywhere. I read some comic books and watched some movies on Netflix.
Larissa: Well, that's fun, too.

5 **Read the dialogue again. Then decide if the sentences are T (true) or F (false).**

a. Larissa had a good weekend. T F
b. Ian stayed at home. T F
c. Larissa doesn't think watching movies is fun. T F
d. Ian went to the movies. T F
e. Larissa slept a friend's house. T F
f. Ian read comic books. T F

6 **Complete these short dialogues.**

a. **A:** My weekend was a lot of fun.
B: Really? What did you do?
A: I hung out with friends.

b. **A:** Gabriela went to the movie theater last night.
B:
A: She watched *Logan* again.

c. **A:** David and I went shopping.
B:
A: We bought an *Atari Flashback Mini*.

d. **A:** Alex and Dylan took a trip last summer.
B:
A: They went to Fortaleza.

DOWNLOADING

7 **Work with a partner. Take turns asking questions about last weekend. Try to find at least three activities in common with your classmate.**

What did you do last weekend?

I went to the beach with my family.

LOADING

1 **Look at the pictures and see what Larissa did last Saturday.**

a.

b.

c.

2 **Look at the pictures in Activity 1 again. Then match them with the sentences below.**

- [ ] **After that** she slept at a friend's house.
- [ ] **First** Larissa and her mother went to the shopping mall.
- [ ] **Then** she hung out with some friends at the park near her house.

Study this

Sequence words

First → Then → After that

UPLOADING

3 **Number the sentences in each group to put the events in order.**

- [ ] After that we looked for the ball in Tom's backyard.
- [ ] On Sunday morning we played soccer in Tom's backyard.
- [ ] Then we searched Tom's neighbors' backyards.
- [ ] Tom kicked the ball very hard and it disappeared.
- [ ] We finally found it in the lake behind Tom's house.
- [ ] We went back to Tom's backyard and started the game again.

- [ ] After I got up, I took a shower.
- [ ] My dad drove for about one hour. Finally, we arrived at the camping site.
- [ ] My dad woke me up very early. It was just after six.
- [ ] On Saturdays I usually get up at 10. But last Saturday was different.
- [ ] Then I had breakfast and packed my backpack.
- [ ] We left our house at 6:30.

4 **Match the pictures with the sentences. Then rewrite the text. Use *first*, *then*, and *after that*.**

a. She found a basketball in front of her house.

b. She jumped happily because the ball went through the hoop.

c. She threw the ball toward the net.

d. She went to the basketball court and started dribbling the ball.

e. Jennifer went outside on a sunny morning.

DOWNLOADING

5 **Write six sentences that describe what you did last Saturday. Use the sequence words *first*, *then*, and *after that*.**

Your turn!

Work with a partner. Read your story to him/her. Did you do anything similar?

LOADING

1 **Louise and Barbara are planning their weekend. Listen and read.**

46

Louise: Hi, Barbara. How's it going?
Barbara: Good, and you?
Louise: I'm fine, thanks. Just a little tired of studying for all the tests we are going to have next week.
Barbara: Me too! What are you up to this weekend?
Louise: Not a lot. Why?
Barbara: Do you want to go and watch that new movie with Chase Crawford?
Louise: Yeah, that sounds good. When?
Barbara: How about Saturday evening?
Louise: Good idea. Do you think we can meet at the mall at 7 p.m.?
Barbara: I'm sorry, I need to take care of my brother until 7:30 p.m. What about 8 p.m.? Can you make it?
Louise: Yes, sure! There is another session at 8 o'clock. Let's watch that one.
Barbara: Great! See you there!

2 **Read the dialogue again. Then underline the correct alternatives.**

a. Louise **has a lot/does not have a lot** to do this weekend.

b. Barbara invites Louise to **go to the movie theater/watch a movie at her house**.

c. The girls will meet on **Saturday/Sunday** evening.

d. Barbara has to take care of her **sister/brother**.

e. The girls decide to meet at **7 p.m./8 p.m.**

3 **Listen again and repeat the dialogue.**

47

Study this

Making Arrangements

Let's + base form	How about/What about + gerund
Let's watch that new movie with...	**How about** having lunch at...?
Let's go to the cafeteria and grab a bite to eat.	**How about** going to the cafeteria before class?
Let's study for the math text.	**What about** going after class? Can you come?

UPLOADING

4 **Complete these short dialogues according to the information given.**

a.

A: How about going to the movie theater this weekend?

B: Yeah, that sounds good. When?

A: On Sunday. At six o'clock.

B: Good idea. ______ the movie theater.

A: ______ See you there!

b.

A: What about going to ______ this weekend?

B: Yeah, that sounds good. When?

A: On ______ after lunch.

B: Good idea. ______ !

A: ______ See you there!

DOWNLOADING

5 **Work with a partner. Arrange a time and a place to meet. Write the arrangement in your diary below. Refer to the dialogues above.**

SATURDAY	SUNDAY
MORNING	MORNING
AFTERNOON	AFTERNOON
EVENING	EVENING

iRead

1 **Read and listen to Zac's description of his school day yesterday.**

READING STRATEGY

48

Hi, there! My name's Zac and I'm from Australia. I'm a typical 13-year-old boy, but I don't go to a typical school. Here's what I did yesterday:

Our school day started at 9:00 a.m. with the school assembly. Our assemblies are different from most school assemblies. We don't listen to people talking about boring, daily topics. In class, we discuss important topics, like bullying, and make decisions about school life. After assembly, I went to my classroom.

In the classrooms, there aren't any desks. Instead, we work around small tables, in groups or individually. First I studied for an hour (we call this an "individual study session"). I did some math exercises and read an interesting text about the history of computers. Then I worked with my classmates Marissa and Jim on a research project. We surfed the Net to find information on the topic, and Ms. Spencer, our tutor, answered some of our questions. Ah, we also listened to our favorite rock band during our research work!

Next, I had P.E. At my school we can choose the sports we want to play. My friends and I played rugby for an hour. It was really fun!

Finally, at 3 o'clock, it was time to go home.

2 **Read the text again and order the events in Zac's school day.**

- [ ] He played rugby with his friends.
- [1] Zac's school day started at 9:00 a.m.
- [ ] He went to his classroom.
- [ ] He worked with his friends on a project.
- [ ] He participated in the school assembly.
- [ ] He did math exercises.
- [ ] He went home.
- [ ] He read a text about the history of computers.

iListen

3 **Listen to Rihanna talking to a friend on the phone about her weekend. These sentences are wrong. Correct them.**

49

a. Rihanna went to the club.

Rihanna went to the beach.

b. She ate pizza and had ice cream.

____

c. She played soccer in the afternoon.

____

d. She had lunch at The Sixties.

____

e. She played video games.

____

1 What are today's teenagers like compared to 25 years ago? Are there any significant differences between the two generations? Which ones? Exchange ideas with your teacher and classmates.

iThink

2 Read the text and check what it says about the questions in Activity 1.

Life as a teenager in 1994, 2014, and 2034 – What a difference a generation makes!

How quickly we forget. Events of decades ago seem like a distant memory, but 1994 was the year when Nelson Mandela was elected President of South Africa, O.J. Simpson was arrested for murder, huge massacres were happening in Rwanda and Sarajevo, and China got its first connection to the Internet. Bill Clinton was President, the Academy Award for Best Picture went to *Forrest Gump*, and the world's population reached 5.6 billion.

To put this year into perspective, this was before the death of Princess Diana (1997).

It was also after the fall of the Berlin Wall (1989), after the Persian Gulf War (1991), after the Rodney King incident (1991), and after the Branch Davidian catastrophe in Waco, Texas (1993).

But most teenagers weren't talking about world affairs. Instead, they were far more interested in getting their driver's license, listening to the music of Madonna, New Kids on the Block, Celine Dion, Coolio, or Prince, or going to the latest Jim Carrey movie.

More telling for these teenagers was what they didn't have yet. They didn't have the Internet, e-mail, smartphones, search engines, social networking, Sony Playstation, Apple iPods, or anything downloadable. Music, movies, and information came on CDs, cassettes, VHS, in cartridges, or in printed form.

But here's one crazy detail you may not have considered. Many of the teens of 1994 are now the parents of teenagers in 2014. This is the group tasked with reinventing the rules of childhood in terms of screen time, cellphone curfews, social networking etiquette, and more. But we're just getting started.

3 Check (✓) the sentences that are true according to the text.

see word pop-up page 170

a. Important events happened in 1994 all over the world, such as China getting its first connection to the Internet. ☐

b. Most teenagers from 1994 were not worried about worldwide issues. ☐

c. Many teenagers of 1994 are parents now, but they are not worried about the use of technological devices. ☐

project

4 What do you understand from this part of the text? Exchange ideas with your classmates.

"More telling for these teenagers was what they didn't have yet. They didn't have the Internet, e-mail, smart phones, search engines, social networking, Sony Playstation, Apple iPods, or anything downloadable. Music, movies, and information came on CDs, cassettes, VHS, in cartridges, or in printed form."

1 Play *Bingo!*

How to play:

- Work in groups of four.
- Write the past forms of the verbs in the box in the bingo grid at random.
- One student calls out the past forms of the verbs.
- He or she can simply say the past (*got up*), or create a sentence using it (*I got up early yesterday.*).
- The first student to get all the verbs in one of the columns is the winner!

DO CLEAN BUY STUDY
HANG OUT PLAY HELP
EAT CHAT HAVE
WASH GO BE
GET UP SEE WATCH

★ BINGO ★

2 How many past forms can you write using the letters in the box? You can repeat letters. You have one minute!

A	D	E	T	W	C
S	H	S	U	Y	I
P	L	N	O	G	V
B	R	M	J	X	K

3 Work in groups of 3. Play *The Last Weekend Game*.

FRIDAY EVENING
2 EAT
3 MISS A TURN
4 DO
5 GO
6 GO BACK THREE SPACES
7 WATCH
8 PLAY
9 HAVE
10 HELP
11 GET UP
12 GO FORWARD TWO SPACES
13 CLEAN
14 MISS A TURN
15 SLEEP
16 MAKE
17 HANG OUT
18 BUY
19 GO BACK TWO SPACES
SUNDAY EVENING

Self-Assessment

Circle the correct alternative to complete the sentences.

1. Thiago usually gets up at 6:30, but last Saturday he **got up/gets up** at 11 o'clock.
2. Ana didn't **hang out/hung out** with friends last weekend. She stayed at home.
3. They **didn't/didn't do** their homework yesterday evening.
4. **A:** What did you do on Sunday evening?
   B: I **eat/ate out**. I went to that new hamburger place on the corner.
5. Bruno didn't ride his bike on the street. He **rode/rides** his bike in the park.
6. **A:** Did the girls **went/go** to the beach or to the countryside?
   B: The girls went to the beach.
7. **A:** Did the boys sleep at a friend's house?
   B: No, they **didn't slept/didn't**.
8. **First/After that** Larissa and her mother went to the shopping mall. Then they had something to eat.
9. **A:** How about going to the movie theater this weekend?
   B: No, I can't./Sounds great. When?
10. **A:** When can we meet?
    B: Outside the movie theater./Is two o'clock OK for you?

What your score means...

8-10 Congratulations! You can understand and use the language learned in this unit.

5-7 Good job! How about looking back over pages 88 to 97? Then answer the questions again.

0-4 Oops... I'm sure you can do better! Let's try again! Go back to pages 88 to 97 and answer the questions. Ask your teacher for help.

1 Read the text and circle the verbs in the Simple Past tense.

THE MOST DECORATED OLYMPIAN OF ALL TIME

By the time he retired at Rio 2016 at the age of 31, Michael Phelps had collected a total of 23 gold, three silver, and two bronze medals at the Olympics, a record-breaking haul that looks unlikely to be bettered for many years to come.

The most decorated athlete of all at Rio 2016, where he won five golds and a silver, Phelps suffered attention deficit/hyperactivity disorder as a child and took up swimming taking at the age of seven to control his energy. Over the years he developed into a champion swimmer, beating record after record in every age category in which he competed.

FROM SYDNEY TO ATHENS

Phelps began to forge his Olympic legend at the age of 15, when he finished fifth in the 200m butterfly final at Sydney 2000. Reflecting on that achievement, the ever-demanding swimmer said: "It was great, I was fifth, that's a pretty big accomplishment."

"There are reasons why I swam every holiday, every Christmas, every birthday," added Phelps, explaining why he was the most dedicated of swimmers. "I was trying to be as prepared as I could, and I tried to see what I could really do and what my potential was. I just really did kind of whatever it took."

Phelps had won five world titles by the time he opened his Olympic account at Athens 2004. Competing in eight events in the Greek capital, he took gold in the 100m and 200m butterfly, 200m and 400m individual medley, and the 4x100m and 4x200m freestyle relays with his U.S.A. teammates. He also won bronze in the 200m freestyle and the 4x100m freestyle relay.

2 Complete the following sentences. Use a verb in the Simple Past and the information in the text.

a. Michael Phelps ________ after ________, when he was 31 years old.

b. During the Olympic Games in 2016 he ________ and ________.

c. Phelps ________ at Sydney in 2000, but he wanted more than that.

d. ________ was the most dedicated swimmer ________ he ________.

3 Unscramble the words and write questions. Then match the questions with the answers.

a. were / born / you / when

b. Ayrton Senna / a / was / car racer

c. they / were / born / where

d. there / many kinds of / video game consoles / were / 1972 / in

e. air pollution / there / in / was / 1960

- [ ] Yes, there was.
- [ ] Yes, he was.
- [ ] On December 3rd.
- [ ] No, there weren't.
- [ ] In a small city near L.A.

4 Rewrite these sentences in order and form a text.

After choosing his clothes, he placed his new pencil case and his notebook in his backpack.
First he chose his clothes and laid them on a chair in his bedroom.
My youngest brother Joshua was excited about his first day at school.
The day before, he had everything ready.
Then he wrote a note for Mom. He wanted her to make a peanut butter sandwich for lunch.

5 Use the prompts below to make arrangements with your friends. Use *Let's…*, *How about…*, and *What about…*

a. watch a movie at your house on Saturday evening

b. study for the history test on Friday afternoon

c. play the new video game tomorrow

unit 7

What did you do last night?

IN THIS UNIT YOU WILL

- talk about past vacation activities
- learn the difference between the Simple Past and the Past Continuous
- describe an action that happened when another action was in progress

START UP

Let's plug in! What kind of game are the people in the picture playing? Do you usually play this kind of game? When? Who do you play with?

LOADING

LEARNING STRATEGY

1 **Nora is telling Mateo about her vacation in July. Listen and read.**

50

Mateo: Hi, Nora! How was your vacation?
Nora: It was good.
Mateo: Really? What did you do?
Nora: I watched some movies and traveled with my grandparents.
Mateo: Great! Where did you go?
Nora: We went to a small town by the beach. They have a house there. We had a very good time. What about you? Where did you go?
Mateo: I didn't go anywhere. But I hung out with some friends and read John Green's books again.
Nora: You're kidding! How many books did you read?
Mateo: Seven.
Nora: I can't believe that! You read seven books in twenty days?
Mateo: That's right. And they were all great.

2 **Read the dialogue again. Then decide if the sentences are T (true) or F (false).**

a. Nora liked her vacation. T F
b. Mateo read a lot during his vacation. T F
c. Both of them traveled last July. T F
d. Mateo read John Green's books. T F
e. Nora traveled to a big city. T F

3 **Listen again and repeat the dialogue.**

51

Grammar feed

Simple Past: Question Words and *Yes/No* Questions

Question Words

What **did** you **do** on your last vacation?
I **watched** some movies and **traveled** with my grandparents.

Where **did** you **go**?
We **went** to a small town by the beach.

How many books **did** you **read**?
I **read** seven books.

***Yes/No* questions**

Did you **travel** on your last vacation?
No, I **didn't**.

Did you **read** seven books in twenty days?
Yes, I **did**.

UPLOADING

4 **Match the questions with the answers.**

a. How did you travel?

b. How many days did you stay with them?

c. What did you do there?

d. When did you come back home?

e. Where did you stay?

f. How much did you pay for the ticket?

We came back last Saturday.

We traveled by plane.

I stayed there for two weeks.

We stayed in a nice hostel.

I walked by the beach, cycled, and met some friends.

We paid $60 per person.

5 **Read the questions and complete the answers.**

a. Did Liz go to the movies yesterday?

No, she didn't. She took care of her little sister.

b. Did they play soccer on Sunday?

No, ______. It rained a lot on Sunday.

c. Did you do your homework?

Yes, ______. It took a long time.

d. Did you and Tyler go to the party?

Yes, ______. We had a great time!

DOWNLOADING

6 **Imagine you are back at school after your summer vacation. Look at the chart and check (✓) the things you did.**

On my vacation, I...	Me	My partner
took a trip.		
went to the movies.		
stayed home.		
played video games.		
read a book.		

Your turn!

Work with a partner. Take turns asking and answering about your vacation.

A: Did you take a trip on your vacation?

B: Yes, I did. / No, I didn't.

A: Where did you go?

B: I went to the beach.

LOADING

1 **Some friends are learning to play a detective game. Listen and read.**

52

Gustavo: Here's how to play the game. One of you stole Mrs. Bishop's jewels. I am the detective and I have to find out who stole them. Look at your card and tell me what you were doing at 7, the time the jewels disappeared. OK?

Ivan: Yes. Let's go.

Gustavo: OK. Ivan, what were you doing at 7?

Ivan: I was cooking in the kitchen.

Gustavo: Cooking, huh? What about you, Andressa? Were you cooking, too?

Andressa: No, I wasn't cooking. I never cook. I was organizing a closet in the master bedroom.

Gustavo: Organizing a closet… What about you, Claudia?

Claudia: I was reading a book in the library.

Gustavo: I see…

2 **Read the dialogue again. Match the people with the activities and rooms.**

Ivan	organize a closet	kitchen
Andressa	read a book	master bedroom
Claudia	cook	library

3 **Listen again and repeat the dialogue.**

53

Grammar feed

Past Continuous

Actions in progress in the past

Affirmative	I **was** cook**ing** in the kitchen.
Negative	I **wasn't** cook**ing**.
Interrogative	**Were** you cook**ing**, too?

UPLOADING

4 **These are other cards from the game. Complete the actions with the verbs from the box. Use the Past Continuous.**

to get up	to eat	~~to organize~~	to study	to update	to watch

Dina Bennet

a. I was organizing the closet.

Dean Lewis

c. I ______ .

Doug Lewis

e. I ______ TV.

Don Benson

b. I ______ the computer.

Dale Bennet

d. I ______ a sandwich.

Dylan Levy

f. I ______ French.

5 **Who stole Mrs. Bishop's jewels? Fill in the spaces with the first letter of each action in Activity 4 and find out.**

D ___ ___ ___ L ___ ___ I ___

DOWNLOADING

6 **Answer the question about you. Write one true answer and one false answer.**

What were you doing at 4 p.m. yesterday?

True answer: ______ False answer: ______

Your turn!

Work with a partner. Take turns asking and answering the question in Activity 6. Can your partner guess which answer is false?

What were you doing at 4 p.m. yesterday?

I was playing video games.

Hmm... I think that's true.

LOADING

1 **It rained heavily last night. Suddenly, at 8 p.m. the lights went off. Look at what these people were doing. Who was in the bathroom?**

2 **Match the people in the apartments to the actions and write sentences.**

a. Lauren was	☐	...cooking dinner.
b. Jessica and Rony were	☐	...reading a book.
c. Nick was	☐	...watching TV.
d. Gabriel was	☐	...taking a shower.
e. Victoria was	☐	...having dinner.
f. Pedro and Marina were	☐	...playing cards.
g. Vincent was	☐	...studying.
h. Fernanda was	☐	...surfing the Net.
i. Sandra was	☐	...brushing his teeth.

UPLOADING

Grammar feed

Past Continuous

Questions words vs. *Yes/No* Questions

What **was** Lauren **doing** at 8 o'clock last night?
She **was watching** TV.

Was Fernanda **having** dinner at 8 o'clock last night?
No, she **wasn't**. She **was cooking**.
Were Pedro and Marina **studying** at that time?
Yes, they **were**.

3 **Look at the pictures and read the questions. Then answer them.**

a. 

Was Barbara eating a piece of cake?

No, she wasn't. She was eating a slice of watermelon.

b. 

Was Josh taking a test?

c. 

Were they playing soccer?

d. 

Were the kids doing their homework?

4 **Answer these questions. Give true answers.**

a. What were you doing at 8 o'clock last night?

b. What was your best friend doing at 10 p.m. last Saturday?

DOWNLOADING

5 **Work with a partner. Play a memory game.**

Step 1: Decide who is going to be Student A and who is going to be Student B.

Step 2: Student B looks at the building on page 110 for 30 seconds. Then he/she closes his/her book.

Step 3: Student A asks questions about the people in the building.

Was Fernanda taking a shower?

No, she wasn't. She was cooking dinner.

LOADING

1 The students and the staff of iLearn Middle School were very busy when the computers crashed yesterday. Look at what they were doing. Who was not using an eletronic device?

The principal was writing an important e-mail.

The school secretary was buying school supplies.

Mr. Hernandez was teaching a Spanish class.

The P.E. teacher was reading some sports news online.

Some students were doing research for a school project.

Juliana was chatting with a friend from China.

UPLOADING

Grammar feed

Past Continuous vs. Simple Past

When the computers **crashed**…
Mr. Hernandez **was teaching** a Spanish class.
some students **were doing** research for a school project.
Juliana **was chatting** with a friend from China.

OR

The computers crashed **while** the P.E. teacher **was reading** some sports news online.
While the school secretary **was buying** school supplies, the computers crashed.

Study this

Use **when** to express that an event occurred at a specific time in the past.
Use **while** to talk about a long action that was happening when a short action interrupted it.

2 **Complete the sentences with the correct form of the verbs in parentheses. Use them in the Past Continuous or the Simple Past.**

a. 

He was skateboarding (to skateboard) when he fell (to fall).

b. 

She ______ (to crash) into a tree while she ______ (to drive).

c. 

While he ______ (to eat), he ______ (to fall) asleep.

d. 

He ______ (to send) a text message when he ______ (to spill) his coffee.

DOWNLOADING

3 **Complete these sentences about you.**

a. When I got up this morning, my ______ was ______.

b. When the bell rang, I ______.

c. When the teacher arrived, ______.

Your turn!

Work with a partner. Share your sentences with him/her. Are they similar or different?

iSkills

iListen

1 **What did you do during your last summer vacation? Share your answer with a classmate.**

iThink

2 **Listen and read some students talking about a great summer vacation they had and complete it with verbs in the past.**

54

Kids share their tales of adventure on summer vacation

We asked students to share their tales of adventure over the summer break. Here are their stories!

My summer vacation started when my mom put me on an airplane to visit my dad in Florida. My dad and I ______ lots of fun things after I arrived in Florida, but my favorite part was when my family and I ______ for a road trip. We started our adventure driving from Gainesville, and our first stop was Savannah. My brother took great pictures from the top of a lighthouse and then we went to the beach and ______ around the city.

– Hunter Holloway, 11

This summer I went to Mexico! I ______ so excited! I was hoping to go to Cancun, but we were really going to the outskirts of a little town called Playa del Carmen. On the second day, we got to swim with the dolphins! Our dolphins' names were "Estrella" and "Martes," which mean "Star" and "Mars." They did all sorts of tricks for us. On the fourth day, we went to Chichen Itza, the famous Mayan ruins! We ______ all about Mayan history and their customs.

– Ariel Kline, 12

I just ______, and did the things that I love to do best, including, taking walks with my dogs, writing, taking photographs, and most importantly spending quality time with my mom and dad. My home life is very blessed and I really do take advantage of that, because not a lot of people can say that they are best friends with their parents. Since it is just us three we love going to concerts, plays, musicals, and drive-ins.

– Samantha Jo Prasnitz, 15

iRead

3 **Read the text again and answer the questions with *H* (*Hunter*), *A* (*Ariel*), or *S* (*Samantha*).**

Who…

a. walked around the city? ☐

b. walked the dogs? ☐

c. spent quality time with his/her family? ☐

d. went on a road trip? ☐

e. swam with dolphins? ☐

1 Malala Yousafazai's life changed when she was shot in Pakistan in 2012. What do you know about this? Exchange ideas with your teacher and classmates.

READING STRATEGY

2 Read this book review and check your guesses.

The Story of Malala: a Girl Who Fought for Education and Was Shot by the Taliban

I come from a country that was created at midnight. When I almost died it was just after midday.

When the Taliban took control of the Swat Valley in Pakistan, one girl raised her voice. Malala Yousafzai stood firm and fought for her right to an education.

On Tuesday, October 9th, 2012, when she was just fifteen, she came close to losing her life. She was shot in the head at close range while on the bus home from school, and many people didn't think she would make it.

Copies of an autobiography by Pakistani schoolgirl Malala Yousafzai, entitled 'I am Malala' are pictured in a book store in London, on October 8, 2013.

Instead, Malala's remarkable recovery has led her on an incredible journey from a secluded valley in northern Pakistan to the United Nations headquarters in New York. At just sixteen years old, she has emerged as an international icon of nonviolent resistance and the youngest recipient of the Nobel Peace Prize.

I Am Malala tells the amazing story of a family displaced by global terrorism, the struggle for girls' education, a father who owned a school and supported his daughter's desire to learn and write, and courageous parents who deeply love their daughter in a culture that values sons more. daughter in a society that prizes sons.

3 Read this part of the text again. What kind of prize did Malala win?

"Instead, Malala's miraculous recovery has taken her on an extraordinary journey from a remote valley in northern Pakistan to the halls of the United Nations in New York. At sixteen, she has become a global symbol of peaceful protest and the youngest-ever Nobel Peace Prize laureate."

see word pop-up page 174

4 Underline the correct alternative according to the book review.

a. Malala was attacked when she was **coming back home from school/driving a bus to school**.

b. She won the Nobel Peace Prize when she was **fifteen/sixteen**.

c. Malala lives in a society that prizes **daughters and sons/sons**.

project

rePlay

1 Play the *Freeze Game*. Follow your teacher's instructions.

2 Can you guess what these people were doing five minutes before the pictures were taken?

a.

c.

b.

d.

3 Play *People watching*. Take notes and report back to class.

Self-Assessment

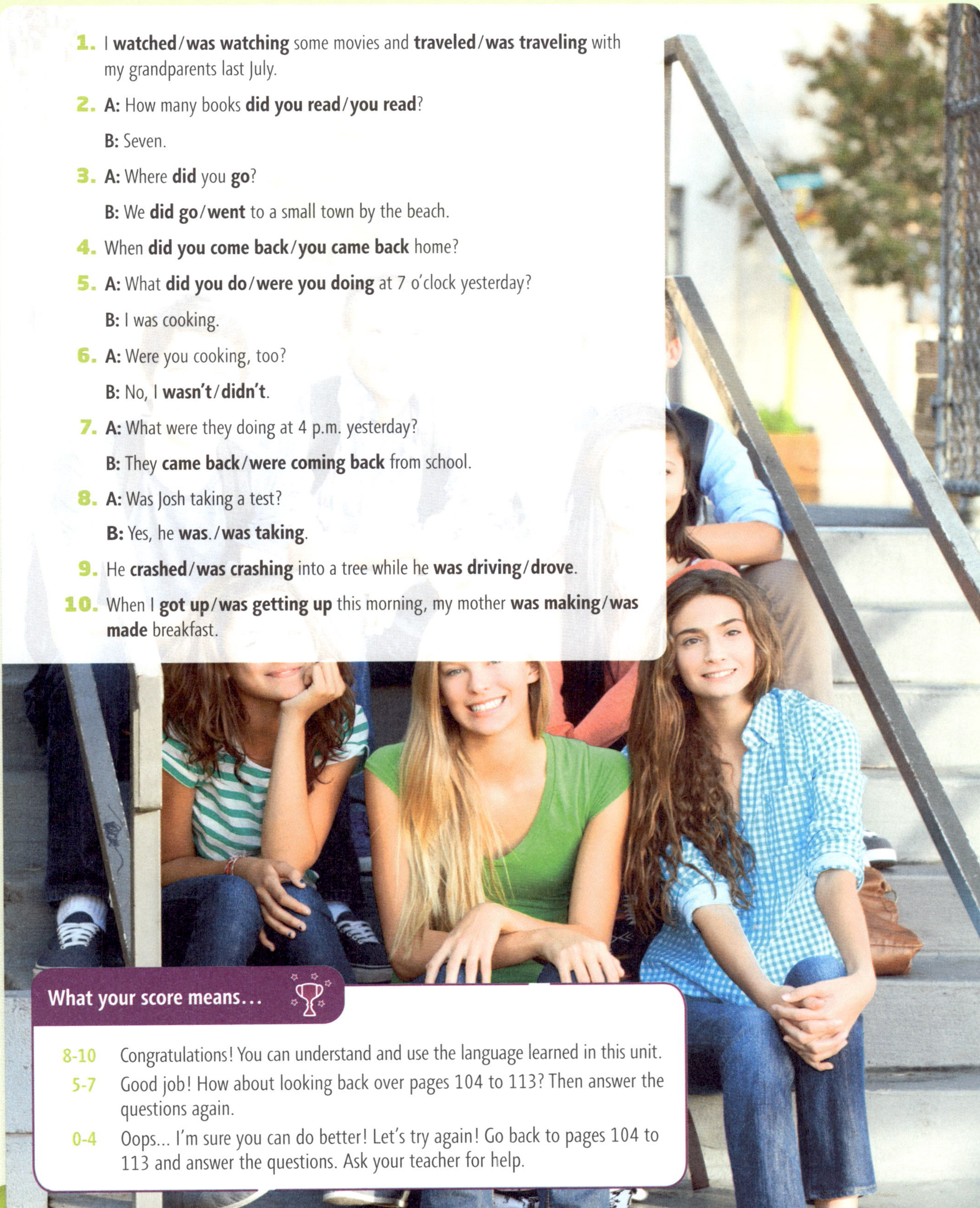

1. I **watched/was watching** some movies and **traveled/was traveling** with my grandparents last July.
2. A: How many books **did you read/you read**?

   B: Seven.
3. A: Where **did** you **go**?

   B: We **did go/went** to a small town by the beach.
4. When **did you come back/you came back** home?
5. A: What **did you do/were you doing** at 7 o'clock yesterday?

   B: I was cooking.
6. A: Were you cooking, too?

   B: No, I **wasn't/didn't**.
7. A: What were they doing at 4 p.m. yesterday?

   B: They **came back/were coming back** from school.
8. A: Was Josh taking a test?

   B: Yes, he **was./was taking**.
9. He **crashed/was crashing** into a tree while he **was driving/drove**.
10. When I **got up/was getting up** this morning, my mother **was making/was made** breakfast.

What your score means...

8-10 Congratulations! You can understand and use the language learned in this unit.

5-7 Good job! How about looking back over pages 104 to 113? Then answer the questions again.

0-4 Oops... I'm sure you can do better! Let's try again! Go back to pages 104 to 113 and answer the questions. Ask your teacher for help.

unit 8 Are you feeling better?

IN THIS UNIT YOU WILL

- learn how to make requests
- talk about health problems and give advice
- express what you like and don't like doing

START UP

Let's plug in! What is going on in the picture? What do you usually do to feel better when you are sick?

LOADING

1 **Amelia is asking her friend Ava for two favors. Listen and read. What favors does she ask?**

55

Amelia: I'm not feeling well. Can you do me a favor, Ava?

Ava: Sure.

Amelia: Can you tell our coach I went home?

Ava: Of course! I'll tell him. Don't worry.

Amelia: Thanks.

Ava: No problem.

Amelia: Oh, and can you text me about the next game?

Ava: Sure! I can come over to your house after the practice, if you don't mind.

Amelia: Great!

Ava: I hope you feel better.

Amelia: Thank you. See you later then.

Ava: See you.

2 **Read the dialogue again. Then check (✓) the true sentences.**

a. Ava is going home. ☐

b. Amelia is not going to practice today. ☐

c. Ava is going to Amelia's house after practice. ☐

d. Amelia is going to Ava's house after practice. ☐

e. Ava is going to text Amelia about the next game. ☐

3 **Listen again and repeat the dialogue.**

56

4 **Amelia is talking to the school bus driver now. Listen and read.**

57

Amelia: Mr. Brown, could you take me home earlier today? I'm not feeling well.

Mr. Brown: Sorry, Amelia. I can't leave now. I'm waiting for some students. But I'm leaving in fifteen minutes. You can come with me then.

Amelia: Can I wait on the bus?

Mr. Brown: Of course you can.

Amelia: Thank you.

Mr. Brown: You're welcome.

Study this

Use *Sure* and *Of course* to agree to do a favor.

Use *Sorry* to refuse to do a favor.

UPLOADING

5 **Write the requests in the correct order.**

a. you / to school / take my homework / Can

Can you take my homework to school?

b. give me / you / that magazine / Could

c. a hot water bottle / Can / you / bring me

d. turn on / you / Can / the TV

e. Could / open / the window / you

Grammar feed

Requests: *Can* and *Could*

Can you **tell** our coach I went home?

Could you **take** me home earlier today?

Study this

Can → informal situation

Could → formal situation

6 **Match the requests in Activity 5 to these replies.**

- [ ] Sure! Do you want that one on the table?
- [ ] Sorry… actually, I'm not going to school tomorrow.
- [ ] Sorry, I need silence. I have to finish my reading now.
- [ ] Sure. It's hot in here!
- [ ] Of course! Is it in the kitchen?

DOWNLOADING

7 **Imagine you are sick at home. A friend is visiting you. What favors can you ask him/her to do for you? Write three ideas below.**

Your turn!

Work with a partner. Take turns asking for favors and agreeing or refusing to do them. Use the ideas from Activity 7.

Could you help me do my homework?

Sorry, I have to study.

LOADING

1 **These people are not feeling well. Look at the pictures, listen, and write.**

58

a. 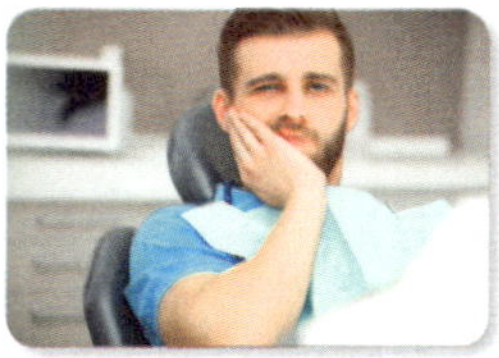

I have a toothache.

b. 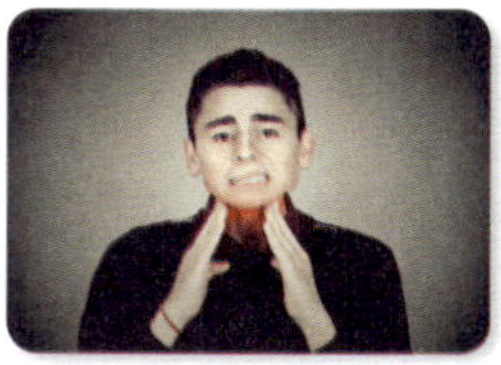

c. 

d. 

e. 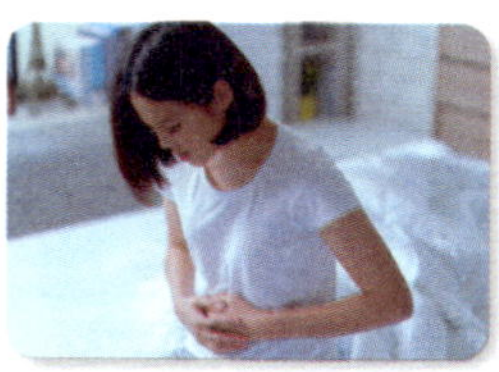

f. 

g. 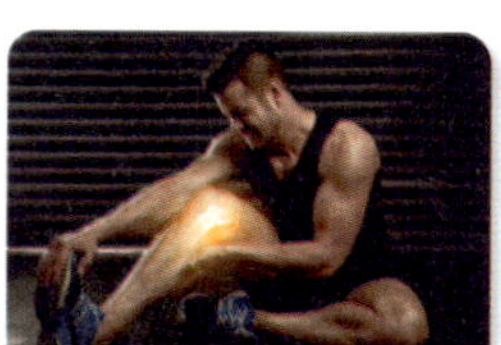

h. 

2 **Look at some things the people from Activity 1 can do to feel better. What are they good for? Match the problems with the possible remedies.**

Drink lots of water.

Problem(s): b, d, and e

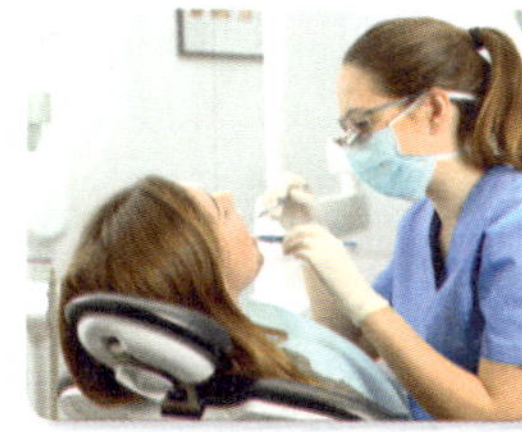

See a dentist.

Problem(s):

Drink tea with honey.

Problem(s):

Use a hot water bottle.

Problem(s):

3 **Amelia is on the bus when a student gets on and talks to her. Listen and read.**

59

Andrea: Hi, Amelia… What's the matter?

Amelia: I'm not feeling very well. I have a terrible headache.

Andrea: Oh, that's too bad. Maybe you should take an aspirin.

Amelia: Well, I'm going home earlier. I'm going to rest.

Andrea: Good idea. I hope you feel better.

4 **Read the dialogue again and answer the questions.**

a. What's Amelia's problem?

b. What does Andrea advise her to do?

5 **Listen again and repeat the dialogue.**

60

UPLOADING

6 **Match the problems with the advice.**

a. I have a headache.

b. John has low grades at school.

c. My dog is restless.

d. Andrea's parents are very strict.

[ ] She should talk to them.

[ ] He should study harder.

[ ] You should take him for a walk.

[ ] So you shouldn't play video games!

Grammar feed

Advice: ***Should***

Affirmative	Maybe you **should take** an aspirin. You **should see** a doctor.
Negative	You **shouldn't play** volleyball today. You **shouldn't go** to school.

Study this

shouldn't = should not

7 **Look at the pictures and complete the sentences. Then write appropriate advice.**

a.

Maria has a stomachache.

Advice: She should see a doctor.

b.

Chao has a bad ________.

Advice: ________.

DOWNLOADING

8 **Work with a partner. Imagine you are not feeling well. Take turns describing your problem and giving advice.**

What's the matter?

I have a cold.

You should go home and rest.

LOADING

1 **Listen and read people talking about what they like doing in their free time.**

61

a.

b.

c.

Grammar feed

***Like*, *Love*, and *Hate* + Gerund**

I **like going** to the movies very much.
In fact, I **hate playing** tennis.
I **love watching** TV. It's my favorite free time activity.

UPLOADING

2 **Complete the sentences with the verbs in parentheses. Use the gerund form.**

a. I like ______ out with my friends on weekends. (to go)

b. She doesn't like playing any sports, but she loves ______ cards. (to play)

c. He hates ______, but he likes washing dishes. (to cook)

d. She loves ______. She swims three days a week. (to swim)

e. They like ______, but they love singing. (to dance)

3 **Write true sentences about you. Use *like*, *love*, and *hate* and the gerund form of the verbs that express the actions in the pictures.**

a. 

I love/ like/ don't like/ hate reading.

b. 

c. 

d. 

e. 

f. 

DOWNLOADING

4 **Work with a partner. Ask him/her about the actions in Activity 3.**

Do you like reading?

Yes, I do. I like reading a lot.

Do you like watching TV?

No, I don't. In fact, I hate watching TV.

LOADING

1 **Listen and read these comic strips.**

62

2 **Listen again and role-play the comic strips.**

63

UPLOADING

3 **Complete the sentences with the correct tense of the verbs in parentheses. Use them in the past, present, or future.**

a. 

A: Can you help me in the kitchen, Mark?

B: Oh, I'm sorry! I can't help you now, Mom. I ______ for the geography test. (to study)

b. 

A: What did the doctor advise you to do, Jessica?

B: He ______ me to take some aspirin. (to advise)

c. 

A: Are you going to my birthday party on Saturday?

B: I think so. I ______ in the basketball championship game in the afternoon, but I don't think it ______ very late. (to play / to finish)

4 **Rewrite the sentences, but keep their meaning. Use *so*.**

a. Because it is raining hard, we are going to stay home.

It is raining hard, so we are going to stay home.

b. Because we did not pay the rent, he told us to vacate the room.

______

c. Because he won't arrive in time, we are going without him.

______

Grammar feed

***So* as a Consequence**

Because I am feeling sick, I'm not going to play golf today. I'm going home.

(I am feeling sick → **reason**; I'm not going to play golf today. I'm going home. → **consequence**)

I am feeling sick, **so** I'm not going to play golf today. I'm going home.

DOWNLOADING

5 **Write two sentences that express consequences. Then share your sentences with a partner.**

______

______

iWrite

1 **Lorena has two new classmates this semester. She wants to go out with them next weekend, so she is texting them and checking what they like doing in their free time. Answer her questions.**

LEARNING STRATEGY

iListen

2 **Aaron is not feeling well. Listen to his conversation with his teacher and choose the correct alternative.**

64

a. What's wrong with Aaron?

- [ ] He has a headache.
- [ ] He has a stomachache.
- [ ] He has a pain in his back.

b. According to the teacher, Aaron shouldn't

- [ ] ...play soccer.
- [ ] ...play basketball.
- [ ] ...do his homework.

c. The teacher advises Aaron to

- [ ] ...see a doctor.
- [ ] ...play soccer.
- [ ] ...go home and rest.

iSpeak

3 **Work with a partner and role-play the dialogue. Use the language from this unit.**

A: What's the matter, ____________________?

B: I have ____________________.

A: You should ____________________.

B: You're right. Could you ____________________, please?

A: ____________________.

1 What do you consider to be healthy habits? Exchange ideas with your classmates.

2 Read the article and check your ideas.

READING STRATEGY

iThink

Dieting: information for teens

If you're a teenager, you constantly see messages telling you to change yourself. You find them everywhere, in magazines, on the Internet, on TV, and in movies. Most of these messages are ads trying to get you to buy things like clothes, makeup, or weight loss products.

The media often tells you that you need to be thin. But in reality, happy and successful people come in all different shapes and sizes.

Besides the pressure to be thin, you also hear about ways to reduce weight. When people talk about 'going on a diet', they usually mean eating less or changing what they eat to lose weight. Dieting can involve good choices like eating more fruits, vegetables, and fiber, or cutting down on snacks. But it can also involve bad choices like skipping meals, eating too little, or not eating a variety of foods.

Here are some healthy suggestions:

- Eat many different kinds of foods each day.
- Have breakfast every morning.
- Eat when you're hungry and stop when you're full.
- Include all four food groups in your meals daily.
- Drink water instead of soda or juice.
- Pick foods high in cereal fiber, like cereal or cereal bars.
- Don't use food to cope with boredom, sadness, or stress.
- Being active is important for your health and happiness. Do something active every day with people you like.

3 Read the article again and check (✓) the true statements.

- [ ] Use food to make yourself feel better.
- [ ] Exercising is important to feel good about yourself.
- [ ] Eat something from all food groups every day.
- [ ] Being successful doesn't depend on your shape or size.
- [ ] You can skip breakfast sometimes.

see word pop-up page 178

project

Work in groups of three. Play *The Review Game*.

START

- Stand up until your next turn.
- Make a prediction about your future.
- Ask a friend what he or she did last summer.
- Smile until your next turn.
- Go back to the beginning of the game.
- Ask a friend to do you a favor.
- Go back one space.
- Tell your classmates what you were doing at 6 p.m. yesterday.
- Don't speak until your next turn.
- Where were you last night?
- Hold a friend's hand until your next turn.
- Miss a turn.
- Tell your classmates what you did last weekend.
- In your opinion, what's the most interesting place in your city?
- Go forward 3 spaces.
- Your classmate has a headache. Give him/her advice.
- Ask a classmate how old he or she is.
- Tell your classmates something you used to do when you were 5 years old.
- Go back one space.
- Keep your hands on your head until your next turn.
- Compare your city to New York.
- Ask two classmates what they were doing last night.
- Draw a water bottle.
- Describe three rules from your school.
- Tell your classmates your plans for your next vacation.
- Go back one space.
- Close your eyes until your next turn.
- Go forward 1 space.

FINISH

Self-Assessment

Circle the correct alternative to complete the sentences.

1. **Can you do/You can do** me a favor, Ava?
2. Mr. Brown, **could you take/you could take** you take me home earlier today?
3. **A:** Can you turn on the TV?
   B: **Sorry/Sure**, I have to study.
4. **A:** Could you give me that newspaper?
   B: **Sorry!/Sure!** Today's newspaper or yesterday's?
5. **A:** I have a **toothache/headache**.
   B: You should take an aspirin.
6. **A:** Alan has a bad **earache/sore throat**.
   B: He should see a doctor then.
7. I'm not feeling well today, **because/so** I'm going home to rest.
8. Ana likes **going/go** out with her friends on weekends.
9. **A:** What do you like **doing/do** on Sunday evenings?
   B: I like staying home and watching TV.
10. You **should drink/drink should** a lot of water.

5

6

What your score means...

8-10	Congratulations! You can understand and use the language learned in this unit.
5-7	Good job! How about looking back over pages 118 to 127? Then answer the questions again.
0-4	Oops... I'm sure you can do better! Let's try again! Go back to pages 118 to 127 and answer the questions. Ask your teacher for help.

Rewind 4 Units 7 - 8

1 Read the conversation. Then write the questions from the box in the correct place.

And how was it?	And who did you meet?	Did you go alone?	
Did you like it?	How long did you stay there?	What did you do there?	Where did you stay?

A: So tell me about your last vacation, Ian.

B: Well, it was in Vietnam.

A: Vietnam? ______

B: I was there for three weeks.

A: ______

B: Much better than I expected, in fact. It's a beautiful country.

A: I'm surprised to hear that. ______

B: Lots of things. In the south, I went to the beach and I went swimming in the ocean. It was very hot. In the north, I went hiking.

A: Oh, really?

B: Yes. It was really beautiful! And there are many different ethnic groups in the north. It was great to meet so many different people.

A: ______

B: No, I went with my family and some friends.

A: Cool. ______

B: We met many families and children. Some were farmers working in the rice fields.

A: ______

B: In a hostel.

A: ______

B: Yes. We usually stay in hostels. They're OK.

A: So would you recommend Vietnam?

B: Sure! It was a wonderful trip.

2 Read this meme. Then write why the police officer stopped the man.

______

______

______

______

3 Read the meme again and choose the correct alternative.

- [ ] The meme explores a current social issue.
- [ ] The meme is humorous.
- [ ] The meme is about drinking and driving.

4 Unscramble the parts and form questions. Then match the questions with the answers.

a. movies / to / like / do / the / going / you

A: ______

b. like / you / tennis / playing / do

A: ______

c. do / like / TV / you / watching

A: ______

d. time / what / free / do / your / you / in / like / doing

A: ______

- [ ] **B:** I love watching TV. It's my favorite free-time activity.
- [ ] **B:** Yes, I like it very much. I always go to the movies.
- [ ] **B:** I like riding my bike in the park.
- [ ] **B:** No, I don't. In fact, I don't like any sports.

5 Match the columns and write sentences. Use *so*.

a. It was raining.

b. We didn't want to miss the show.

c. Anne forgot her watch.

- [ ] We hurried to the theater.
- [ ] We didn't know the time.
- [ ] We canceled the picnic.

a. It was raining, so we canceled the picnic.

b. ______

c. ______

6 What should these people do? Read about their problems and give them some advice.

a. I have a fever. ______

b. I have a pain in my back. ______

c. I have a sore throat. ______

READING HUB

READING HUB

1 These are some signs used in Ontario, Canada. Do you know what they mean? Are they similar to the signs in your country? Why are signs important?

2 Read the text and check your predictions.

READING STRATEGY

SIGNS

Traffic signs provide essential details about rules, alert you about dangerous conditions, and guide you on your route. They use different symbols, colors, and shapes to be easily recognized.

Here are some of the many signs you will see on Ontario roads:

A stop sign has eight sides and it is red with white letters. It means you need to stop completely. If there's a stop line on the road, stop there. If not, stop at the crosswalk. If there's no crosswalk, stop at the edge of the sidewalk. What if there's no sidewalk? Then stop at the edge of the intersection. Only go when it's safe and the road is clear.

A school zone sign has five sides and a bright yellow/green background with black symbols. It alerts you that you're near a school area. If you see this sign, slow down, be extra careful, and watch for children.

Regulatory signs

These signs tell you what you must do. Typically, they are rectangular or square in shape and feature a white or black background with letters in black, white, or various colors. If a sign displays a green circle, it signifies that you should or must perform the action shown within the circle. On the other hand, a red circle with a diagonal line indicates that the activity is prohibited.

Here are some common regulatory signs:

This road is an official bike route. Look out for cyclists and be ready to share the road with them.

You may park in the area between the signs during the times posted. (Signs are used in pairs or groups.)

Do not enter this road.

see word pop-up page 150

3 According to the text, what's the difference between a sign with a green circle and a red circle with a line through the sign?

1 What do you know about Bill Gates? Did you know he is good at predicting the future? Do you know any of his predictions for the future?

2 Read the text and find out.

Bill Gates may be living in the present, but his mind is always focused on the future. He has built his career by forecasting developments in computing, public health, and the environment.
He correctly predicted the growth of smartphones and social media, and there's plenty of evidence indicating that his latest predictions might also be accurate.

Here's what Gates envisions for the future of our world.

- Bioterrorism could wipe out 33 million people in less than a year.
  [...]
- When it comes to food, Africa will become entirely self-sufficient.
  [...]
- Mobile banking will help the poor transform their lives.
  [...]
- By 2030, the world will discover a clean-energy breakthrough to power our world.
  [...]
- Countless jobs will be lost to automation.
  [...]

see word pop-up page 154

3 Do you think his predictions will come true? Why? Why not? In small groups, discuss them.

Reading Hub

1 **Have you ever heard of the U.S. city Seattle? What do you know about it? Read the text about some places tourists visit there. Would you like to visit them? Give reasons.**

READING STRATEGY

Top Things to do in Seattle

People say that it rains a lot in Seattle. Sure, a rain jacket is useful. But Seattle's total annual rainfall is actually less than a number of other U.S. cities. When you're in the Emerald City, you'll be thankful for the regular mists and accompanying mild climate; they make Seattle one of the greenest cities around.

But visitors to Seattle don't just flock here for the great outdoors. They come for the music, culture, lifestyle, coffee, and attractions. If you're planning a trip to the Emerald City, here's a list of the most popular things to do in Seattle.

Space Needle

Since its construction for the 1962 Seattle World's Fair, the Space Needle has become both an internationally recognized icon and Seattle's most popular attraction.

Pacific Science Center

Celebrating its 50th anniversary in 2012 (the Space Needle also turned 50 in 2012), the Pacific Science Center continues to engage visitors – especially young ones – through a variety of personal experiences.

Space Museum of Pop Culture

Formerly called Experience Music Project | Science Fiction Museum, the dramatic, fluid lines of the Frank O. Gehry-designed building that houses both museums is a must-see in and of itself. Inside you'll find leading-edge and award-winning exhibitions that celebrate the creative process and popular culture. [...]

2 **Read the sentence and choose a synonym for the underlined word.**

But visitors to Seattle don't just <u>flock</u> here for the great outdoors.

☐ go somewhere in large numbers ☐ disappear quickly

see word pop-up page 158

3 **Choose one place most tourists visit in your city and write a short description of it. Use the language learned in the unit. You can also use a dictionary.**

1 Do you recognize these sports? Are they dangerous? How can we do them in a safe way? Exchange ideas with your teacher and classmates.

READING STRATEGY

2 Read the text about some extreme sports in South America. Which one would you like to try?

Extreme Sports Adventures in South America

Although it's not the capital of or the largest city in Colombia, Medellin is a favorite of many travelers. Many tourist companies offer rides to the tourists that want to see the city from above. The flights generally take 25 or 30 minutes and provide a spectacular view of entire Medellin valley and the west near Santa Fe de Antioquia.

Giant sand dunes are not the first thing that comes to people's mind when they think of South America. However, the subcontinent is vast, with different types of ecosystems including dry, arid land in Peru. The local operators will take you out in dune buggies to explore the land and find the right hill.

Kayaking is popular in Chile as there are hundreds of glacial lakes and crystal clear rivers. Guided tours are offered that last from two to nine days. It is recommended that you choose a guided tour as the land is still relatively untouched. This way you will avoid running into problems. It is possible to kayak through Chile's Lake District to Northern Patagonia unguided, however.

Mindo is only an hour and a half from Quito, just before reaching one of Ecuador's many rainforests. The valley is very popular with birdwatchers as there are more than 500 species of birds. There is also a variety of plants and other wildlife. There are many trails and waterfalls to visit. Ziplining in the Mindo is amazing. As you are carried across horizontal cables, you have a spectacular view of the area.

see word pop-up page 162

3 Discuss these questions with a classmate.

- What did you learn about the extreme sports in each country?
- Would you like to visit one of those places? Which one? Why?
- What extreme sports can you do in Brazil? Can you remember in which part of Brazil people do these sports?

1 **Have you ever heard of Martin Luther King? What is his memorable statement? Exchange ideas with your teacher and classmates.**

see word pop-up page 166

2 **Read the first page of the book *Martin Luther King* and answer the questions that follow.**

a. What happened on August 28th, 1963 in Washington, D.C.?

b. Who participated in the march?

c. What did they want?

d. Who was there to talk to the people?

e. Did Martin prepare his speech?

f. Did he use the speech he prepared?

g. What was his dream?

"I HAVE A DREAM"

On August 28, 1963, Martin Luther King, Jr.* stood in front of more than 250,000 protest marchers in Washington, D.C. and gave one of the most famous speeches in US history. This protest march was the largest demonstration in the US at that time. About 60,000 marchers were white people; the other marchers were black. They came from all parts of the country into the nation's capital because they wanted change. They wanted equality for all Americans.

In the weeks before this march, the organizers invited important speakers. King worked on his speech all night, trying to find the right words. But the next day, in the middle of his speech, he changed it. He looked up at the crowd and spoke about his dream for America:

"I have a dream today . . . one day little black boys and little black girls will be able to join hands with little white boys and little white girls as sisters and brothers."

King's dream has not come true yet. But many Americans today have the same dream. His fight for peace, equality, and freedom for all people continues.

*Jr.: short for "Junior." This word is used after a man's name when he has the same name as his father.

3 **Martin Luther King's "fight for peace, equality, and freedom for all people" contributed positively to today's American civil rights. Think of someone who was important to your country's development. Why were they important? Exchange ideas with your classmates.**

1 **Do you like reading comic strips? Why? How often do you read them? Have you ever heard of Garfield? Exchange ideas with your teacher and classmates.**

2 **Read the comic strip below and do the activities.**

see word pop-up page 170

a. These are Garfield's answers to Jon's questions in scenes 1 and 2: "I scratched it." and "I ate it." Which verb is regular and which one is irregular? How do you know that?

b. What did Garfield do? Match the verbs to the objects.

1. destroy ☐ record

2. eat ☐ fern

3. scratch ☐ lasagna

c. Complete the sentences. Use sequence words.

______ Garfield scratched Jon's record. ______ he ate Jon's lasagna. ______ he destroyed Jon's fern.

d. Why does Jon shout 'CATS!'? Check (✓) the correct answer.

☐ Because he wants Garfield to come to him.

☐ Because he saw some cats walking.

☐ Because he is angry.

1 After surviving catastrophes, what do the survivors usually tell others? Do you know anybody who has survived a catastrophe? Who is he/she? What did he/she tell you about it? Share with your teacher and classmates.

2 Read this survivor's story and answer the questions.

Hari, 65, was in her field when the earthquake happened. It knocked her down and left her family of 15 homeless. Now, they are living in a temporary tent with a tarp that Mercy Corps gave them in an emergency kit.

"The earthquake happened right after lunch. We were in our fields. The young children were playing outside the house. We couldn't take anything from our houses because we were already outside. We were shaken and couldn't stand up. Everything around us was shaking and there was dust everywhere."

Their house is still standing, but only just, and they haven't changed clothes since the earthquake occurred. Although there are some clothes and food inside, they are too frightened to enter, fearing that another tremor could cause it to collapse. Hari says she's just worried about how to survive day-to-day life.

a. How many people in her family suffered the consequence of the earthquake?

see word pop-up page 174

b. Was Hari at home when the earthquake hit them?

c. Why didn't they go inside their house?

1 Do you usually use natural remedies? What for? Do you buy them or do you prepare them at home? Are they more effective than industrially-produced remedies? Exchange ideas with your teacher and classmates.

2 Read this recipe and write T (true) or F (false).

Cold-fighting juice

This is truly the ultimate cold and flu tonic. Combining vitamin C-rich citrus fruits with immune modulating herbs and a little fat makes this a powerful option. The ingredients are simple enough:

- 1 **tablespoon** dried ginger
- ¼ cup fresh turmeric root
- 1 orange, peeled
- 1 lemon, peeled
- 1 **teaspoon** honey
- Water as needed

Place all ingredients through your juicer or your **blender**. Blend until smooth. Drink a cup of this vitamin C rich juice every two hours alongside a healthy dose of rest and your immune system will be giving you a warm hug of thanks, in the form of good health.

a. The recipe uses four fruits. T F

b. You will only use water if necessary. T F

c. This recipe is good for headaches. T F

d. The writer recommends that you drink two cups an hour. T F

see word pop-up page 178

3 Look at some measuring tools for kitchens. Match the words in bold in the recipe with the pictures.

Irregular verbs

Base form	Past form	Past Participle	Translation
awake	awoke	awaken	acordar
be	was, were	been	ser, estar
become	became	become	tornar-se
begin	began	begun	começar
bend	bent	bent	dobrar
bet	bet	bet	apostar
bite	bit	bitten	morder
blow	blew	blown	soprar
break	broke	broken	quebrar
bring	brought	brought	trazer
build	built	built	construir
burn	burnt/burned	burnt/burned	queimar
buy	bought	bought	comprar
catch	caught	caught	pegar
choose	chose	chosen	escolher
come	came	come	vir
cut	cut	cut	cortar
do	did	done	fazer
draw	drew	drawn	desenhar
dream	dreamed/dreamt	dreamed/dreamt	sonhar
drink	drank	drunk	beber
drive	drove	driven	dirigir
eat	ate	eaten	comer
fall	fell	fallen	cair
feed	fed	fed	alimentar
feel	felt	felt	sentir
fight	fought	fought	lutar
find	found	found	achar
fly	flew	flown	voar
forget	forgot	forgotten	esquecer
forgive	forgave	forgiven	perdoar
get	got	got/gotten	conseguir
get up	got up	got up/ gotten up	levantar-se
give	gave	given	dar
go	went	gone	ir
grow	grew	grown	crescer
hang out	hung out	hung out	passar tempo
have	had	had	ter
hear	heard	heard	ouvir
hide	hid	hidden	esconder
hit	hit	hit	atingir
hold	held	held	segurar
hurt	hurt	hurt	machucar
keep	kept	kept	manter

Base form	Past form	Past Participle	Translation
know	knew	known	saber, conhecer
lean	leant/leaned	leant/leaned	inclinar-se
learn	learnt/learned	learnt/learned	aprender
leave	left	left	deixar, sair
lend	lent	lent	emprestar
let	let	let	deixar
lose	lost	lost	perder
make	made	made	fazer
mean	meant	meant	significar
meet	met	met	encontrar
overcome	overcame	overcome	superar
pay	paid	paid	pagar
put	put	put	colocar
read	read	read	ler
ride	rode	ridden	andar de
ring	rang	rung	tocar
rise	rose	risen	subir, aumentar
run	ran	run	correr
say	said	said	dizer
see	saw	seen	ver
sell	sold	sold	vender
send	sent	sent	enviar
set	set	set	estabelecer
show	showed	shown	mostrar
sing	sang	sung	cantar
sit	sat	sat	sentar
sleep	slept	slept	dormir
speak	spoke	spoken	falar
spell	spelled/spelt	spelled/spelt	soletrar
spend	spent	spent	gastar, passar tempo
split	split	split	dividir
stand up	stood up	stood up	ficar de pé
steal	stole	stolen	roubar
swim	swam	swum	nadar
take	took	taken	pegar, tomar
teach	taught	taught	ensinar
tell	told	told	contar
think	thought	thought	pensar
throw	threw	thrown	jogar
understand	understood	understood	entender
wake up	woke up	waken up	acordar
wear	wore	worn	vestir
win	won	won	ganhar
write	wrote	written	escrever

WORKBOOK

WORKBOOK

Grammar Reference

SIMPLE PRESENT vs. PRESENT CONTINUOUS

Katherine **usually plays** the electric guitar in her bedroom.

Today, Katherine **is playing** the electric guitar with her band. They **are performing** in the auditorium.

Para falar sobre ações no presente, usamos dois tempos verbais: o ***Simple Present*** e o ***Present Continuous***.

Conjugamos o verbo no ***Simple Present*** quando queremos indicar que um estado ou uma ação acontece sempre, é habitual ou rotineiro, ou ainda para expressar uma verdade que não muda.

Em contrapartida, usamos o ***Present Continuous*** para expressar ações que estão em progresso no presente, acontecendo no momento em que falamos.

Importante:

- No ***Simple Present***, é comum usarmos advérbios que indicam a frequência com que realizamos uma ação. Alguns exemplos dessas palavras são ***usually*** e ***generally*** (geralmente), ***always*** (sempre), ***sometimes*** (às vezes) e ***never*** (nunca).

Agora faça a atividade 1.

ASKING FOR PERMISSION: *CAN*

A: Ms. Evans, **can** I go to the board, **please**?
B: Yes, you **can**.

A: Mom, **can** I use my cell phone now?
B: No, **you can't**. You have to finish your homework.

Usamos ***can*** quando queremos pedir permissão a alguém para fazer algo.

Formar frases com esse verbo é muito simples. Ele tem a mesma forma para todas as pessoas do discurso e, depois dele, empregamos o verbo principal na ***base form*** (no infinitivo sem ***to***).

Na negativa, usamos ***cannot*** (formal) ou a forma contraída ***can't*** (mais comum). Na interrogativa, invertemos a posição entre ***can*** e o sujeito.

Importante:

- Quando pedimos permissão, é aconselhável utilizarmos a palavra ***please*** (por favor). Ela indica boas maneiras.

Agora faça a atividade 2.

ABILITY: *CAN*

Sarah **can** play the tambourine very well.

Josh **can't** play the piano, but he **can** play the drums.

Usamos o verbo ***can*** também para indicar habilidades que temos, algo que conseguimos ou não conseguimos fazer.

Agora faça a atividade 3.

1 Complete the sentences with the Simple Present or Present Continuous.

a. Ed Sheeran is singing a song now. He sings very well. (to sing)

b. He ________ the guitar now. He ________ every day. (to play)

c. Ed ________ at the moment. He always ________ to reporters. (to clap/to talk)

d. Now he ________ for pictures. He ________ pictures with fans. (to pose/to take)

2 Match the questions to the answers.

a. Can I use my cell phone?

b. Excuse me, sir. Can I take pictures here?

c. Can I take my dog to the mall?

d. Can we play the tambourine here?

e. Can I eat my sandwich now?

[ ] Of course you can. Are you hungry?

[ ] No, you can't. Dogs are not allowed in the stores.

[a] Yes, you can. But don't talk for too long.

[ ] I'm sorry. You can't take pictures in the museum.

[ ] No, you can't. You can't make noise in the library.

3 Now answer the questions about you.

a. Can you play a musical instrument or sing in English? ________

b. Can you play volleyball? ________

iCan

Check (✓) the box that best describes your performance in this unit.

1. I can talk about events happening at this moment.	[ ] Yes, I can.	[ ] Not sure.
2. I can talk about habits and routine.	[ ] Yes, I can.	[ ] Not sure.
3. I can ask and give permission using *can*.	[ ] Yes, I can.	[ ] Not sure.
4. I can ask and answer about abilities using *can*.	[ ] Yes, I can.	[ ] Not sure.

We're going to see an exhibition.

FUTURE: *BE GOING TO*

A: Is Sarah **going to** visit her uncle next holiday?
B: No, she **isn't**. She **is going to** stay with her grandparents.

Affirmative

Singular	Plural
I am going to	We are going to
You are going to	You are going to
He/She/It is going to	They are going to

Contractions
I'm-You're-He's-She's-It's-We're-You're-They're

Negative

Singular	Plural
I am not going to	We are not going to
You are not going to	You are not going to
He/She/It is not going to	They are not going to

Contractions
are not - 're not/ aren't   is not - 's not/ isn't

Interrogative

Am	I going to...?	Are	we going to...?
Is	he going to...?		you going to...?
	she going to...?		they going to...?
	it going to...?		

Em inglês, quando queremos falar sobre ações futuras planejadas ou quase certas, usamos ***be + going to***. Para formar essa estrutura na afirmativa, basta conjugar o ***to be*** no ***Simple Present***, acrescentar ***going to*** e, em seguida, o verbo principal na ***base form***.

Na negativa, utilizamos ***to be*** seguido de ***not*** ou suas formas contraídas.

Na interrogativa, invertemos a posição entre ***to be*** e o sujeito. O restante da estrutura permanece igual.

Importante:
- Respondemos a ***yes/no questions*** usando as formas contraídas de ***to be***, sem o restante da estrutura nas respostas negativas somente..

Agora faça as atividades 1 e 2.

FUTURE WITH *BE GOING TO*: QUESTIONS

A: How long are your parents **going to stay** in London?
B: They **are going to stay** there for one week.

Formar perguntas com ***to be + going to*** é muito simples. A ***question word*** fica no início da pergunta. O restante segue a mesma estrutura das ***yes/no questions***.

Algumas das ***question words*** mais comuns são:
- ***what***: o que ou qual (quais);
- ***who***: quem;
- ***where***: onde;
- ***when***: quando;
- ***how***: como;
- ***how long***: quanto tempo ou por quanto tempo.

Agora faça a atividade 3.

OBLIGATIONS: *HAVE TO* AND *DON'T HAVE TO*

A: Does Mark **have to** make his bed every day?
B: Yes, he **does**.

Usamos ***have to*** para indicar obrigações, geralmente que outras pessoas atribuem a nós.

Na afirmativa, há duas formas: ***have to*** (para ***I***, ***you***, ***we*** e ***they***) e ***has to*** (para ***he***, ***she*** e ***it***). Ambas são seguidas do verbo principal.

Na negativa, essa estrutura expressa a falta de obrigatoriedade de realizar uma ação. Para formá-la, usamos os auxiliares ***do*** seguido de ***not*** (ou a forma contraída ***don't***) para ***I***, ***you***, ***we*** e ***they***; e ***does*** (ou a contração ***doesn't***) para ***he***, ***she*** e ***it***.

Na interrogativa, basta empregar a seguinte estrutura: ***do*** ou ***does*** + sujeito + ***have to*** + verbo principal.

Faça a atividade 4.

SO FOR CONSEQUENCES

Ashley got an A on her math test, **so** her parents are very proud.

Assim como em português, em inglês existem diversas conjunções (***conjunctions***), palavras que conectam as orações para que elas façam sentido.

Nesta unidade, você conheceu a conjunção ***so***. Ela introduz uma oração que expressa uma consequência ou um resultado do que afirmamos na oração anterior.

Agora faça a atividade 5.

Word pop-up

admission – entrada	**allowed** – permitido
available – disponível	**crosswalk** – faixa de pedestres
arranged – organizada(s)/o(s)	**law** – lei
courtyard – jardim	**obeyed** – obedecido
foreigner – estrangeiro	**pavement** – chão, pavimento
to request – solicitar	**sidewalk** – calçada
wishing – que desejar(em)	**to warn** – avisar, prevenir

1 These are Felipe's plans for next week. Look at the words and the pictures. Then write sentences using *be going to*.

a. He is going to study for a test.
b.
c.
d.
e.

2 Look at the pictures and guess what this teenager is going to do on her next vacation. Then answer the questions using short answers.

a. Is she going to travel to Rio de Janeiro?
Yes, she is.
b. Is she going to make cupcakes?
c. Is she going to listen to music?
d. Is she going to read a book?
e. Is she going to stay at a hotel?

3 **Read the blog page with people's plans while visiting California. Then write questions to the answers.**

VISIT CALIFORNIA

My sister and I are going to visit the Golden Gate Bridge in San Francisco. She's going to ride a bike and I'm going to walk. I'm a skater, but I am not going to skateboard there because skateboards are not allowed on the bridge.

Denise, 13
Tourist from New Zealand

I'm going to travel to California with my family. We're going to stay there for two weeks and visit the famous Santa Monica beach. I'm going to take a ride on the Ferris wheel. My brother and my mom are going to swim in the sea and my father is going to surf. There is a fun activity for everyone in California!

Estela, 13
Tourist from Costa Rica

I'm going to travel to Los Angeles on my next vacation. My father and I are not going to go to the beaches. We like city life, so we're going to visit the movie studios in L.A. I love movies and TV series, so I'm going to take lots of pictures there.

Bruno, 12
Tourist from Brazil.

My favorite place in California is Los Angeles. I'm going to eat a hamburger in a famous restaurant and visit the Hollywood Walk of Fame. I'm going to try to find the stars of my favorite singers and actors. It's going to be fun!

Lucca, 14
Tourist from Italy

I like computer and mobile technology. I want to be a game developer when I grow up. During my trip to California, I'm going to visit Silicon Valley. That's where most of the technology companies are.

Pedro, 13
Tourist from Portugal

a. [Who] is going to visit Santa Monica beach?
Estela.

b. [ ] is Bruno going to see the movie studios?
In Los Angeles.

c. [ ] place is Pedro going to visit?
Silicon Valley.

d. [ ] is Denise's sister going to cross the Golden Gate Bridge?
By bike.

e. [ ] is Estela going to be in California?
For two weeks.

f. [ ] is Lucca going to try to find in Los Angeles?
The stars of his favorite singers and actors.

g. [ ] is Bruno going to travel to California?
On his next vacation.

4 Look at the table. Then write sentences about Kevin and Diana.

	to get up early	to finish the geography project	to make the bed	to clean the bedroom	to study for a history test	to visit a friend in hospital
 Kevin	✓		✓	✓	✓	
 Diana		✓	✓			✓

Kevin

Kevin has to get up early.

______

______

______

______

______

Diana

Diana doesn't have to get up early.

______

______

______

______

______

5 Match the columns to form sentences.

a. It is very hot here,
b. We don't have school tomorrow,
c. It's raining,
d. I'm too tired to walk,
e. I have some extra money,
f. We're going to be late for class,

☐ so let's hurry up.
☐ so let's take the bus.
☐ so let's play video games all day long.
☐ so let's take an umbrella.
☐ so let me pay for the ice cream.
☐ so let's turn on the air-conditioning.

iCan

Check (✓) the box that best describes your performance in this unit.

1. I can talk about plans for the future. ☐ Yes, I can. ☐ Not sure.
2. I can talk about obligations. ☐ Yes, I can. ☐ Not sure.
3. I can talk about consequences. ☐ Yes, I can. ☐ Not sure.

Will things be different then?

Grammar Reference

SPONTANEOUS DECISIONS AND OFFERS: *WILL*

A: It's so cold in here!
B: Don't worry. I **will** close the window.

Para falar sobre decisões imediatas, ou seja, decisões que foram tomadas no momento em que estamos falando, usamos ***will***.

Agora faça as atividades 1 e 2.

PREDICTIONS ABOUT THE FUTURE: *WILL*

Robots **will** cook for people in the year 3000.

Affirmative

Singular		Plural	
I / You / He / She / It	will	We / You / They	will
Contractions: I'll - You'll - He'll - She'll - It'll		**Contractions:** We'll - You'll - They'll	

Negative

Singular		Plural	
I / You / He / She / It	will not/ won't	We / You / They	will not/ won't

Interrogative

Will	I...? / he ...? / she ...? / it ...? / we...? / you...? / they...?

Quando queremos falar de previsões sobre o futuro, usamos ***will***.

Na afirmativa, esse verbo assume a mesma forma para todas as pessoas.

A forma negativa desse modal é ***will not*** ou as contrações ***'ll not*** e ***won't***.

Na interrogativa, invertemos a posição entre ***will*** e o sujeito. Para formar ***question words***, basta começarmos com a ***wh- word***.

Agora faça as atividades 3 e 4.

BE GOING TO vs. *WILL*

I think I **will** travel to Canada next month.
I **am going to** travel to Canada next month. My mother has the tickets for the trip.

Em inglês, podemos usar ***will*** e ***be going to*** para falar sobre o futuro, mas eles têm significados um pouco diferentes.

Usamos ***will*** quando falamos de um futuro incerto, quando planejamos algo, mas não temos certeza se isso ocorrerá.

Em contrapartida, quando usamos ***be going to***, queremos dizer que algo foi planejado ou que certamente acontecerá. Empregamos essa estrutura também para expressar a intenção de fazer ou não algo.

Agora faça as atividades 5 e 6.

Word pop-up

slumber party – festa na qual um grupo de amigos se reúne e dorme na casa de um deles

a wealth of – uma grande quantidade de

breakthrough – inovação, avanço

rise – aumento

to wipe out – destruir

entirely – completamente

countless – inúmeros(as)

brain – cérebro

to gain - ganhar

valuable - valioso(a)

to keep in mind - ter em mente

loneliness - solidão

misconception - equívoco

1 Match the pictures with the sentences from the box.

~~I'll close the window.~~	I'll get you some water.	I'll lend you my glasses.
I'll answer it.	I'll help you carry it.	I'll open it for you.

a.

I'll close the window.

b.

c.

d.

e.

f.

2 Now it's up to you. Say what you will do in each situation.

a. There's a new movie on! I really want to see it!

I'll buy the tickets.

b. It's raining and you need to go to school.

c. There is a geography test next week and you need a good grade.

d. Your mother is carrying a lot of shopping bags.

3 Read the text and write T (true) or F (false).

FUTURE THINGS TO COME

Holografic Pets

Holographic Pets become the next "thing" – interactive AI (Artificial Intelligence) holograms that express and respond to emotions.

Smart Clothing

Special fabrics and tiny electronics make "smart clothing" that changes color and shape, and keeps you cool or warm according to the weather condition.

3D Printing in Every Home

Cheap 3D printing in every home can print out almost anything – electronics, furniture, food, and medicine – using files purchased and downloaded from the Internet.

Edible Robots

Consumable microbots (micro + robots) that repair our injuries from inside our bodies.

a. Clothes will change colors by themselves. T

b. We will eat microrobots when we are sick. ___

c. Zoo animals will be available in each home. ___

d. It will be possible to print 3D pets. ___

e. We will print 3D furniture at home. ___

f. Smart clothing will control our body temperature according to the weather. ___

g. It will be expensive to use a 3D printer at home. ___

h. Pets will interact with us through Artificial Intelligence. ___

4 Make predictions about your future.

LIFE IN 2035

How old will you be?

___

Will you have a college degree?

___

Where will you live?

___

I will speak... Portuguese ☐ Spanish ☐ English ☐ Mandarin ☐

Other: ___

People will travel by...

flying cars. ☐ electric cars. ☐

solar-powered cars. ☐ subway only. ☐

Other: ___

I will...	I won't...

5 Read the dialogue and circle the correct verb forms.

Luana: Ryan, what **are you going to do/will you do** next Saturday?

Ryan: I **am going to go/will go** to a rock concert. I have two tickets. Would you like to come?

Luana: I don't think so. We have a math test on Monday and I **am going to study/will study** on the weekend.

Ryan: Math test? It's not this Monday. It's in two weeks from now.

Luana: Really? Oh, that's great! Then I **am going to go/will go** to the concert with you.

Ryan: Cool! And I **am going to help/will help** you next week. We can study together.

Luana: Thanks, Ryan! You're a great friend.

6 Circle the correct option. Then complete the sentences.

a. What ______ do on Sunday morning?
will you — are you going to

b. I guess I ______ with you to the library. I need to study too.
'll go — am going to go

c. Bye, Ron! I ______ you later.
'll see — am going to see

d. When ______ arrive?
is the teacher going to — will the teacher

e. I promise I ______ late anymore.
won't be — am not going to be

f. I am going to the mall. It's Mayara's birthday on Tuesday. I ______ a gift her.
will buy — am going to buy

iCan

Check (✓) the box that best describes your performance in this unit.

1. I can use *will* to talk about immediate decisions. ☐ Yes, I can. ☐ Not sure.
2. I can use *will* to make predictions. ☐ Yes, I can. ☐ Not sure.
3. I can use *be going to* to emphasize a present intention, certainty, or a plan. ☐ Yes, I can. ☐ Not sure.
4. I can ask and answer about future actions. ☐ Yes, I can. ☐ Not sure.

Workbook unit 3 — This place is more interesting!

COMPARATIVES: SUPERIORITY

Beijing, China, is **noisier than** Fernandina Beach, U.S.A.
Beijing is **more populous than** Fernandina Beach.

Usamos o comparativo de superioridade para compararmos elementos, indicando que um é mais que outro.

Em inglês, formamos esse comparativo de duas maneiras:
- com adjetivos de uma sílaba, adicionamos ***-er*** ao final da palavra, que é, na maioria das vezes, seguida de ***than***;
- com adjetivos de duas ou mais sílabas, usamos ***more* + adjetivo + *than***.

Importante:
- em adjetivos de apenas uma sílaba e que terminam em **consoante + vogal + consoante** (CVC), dobramos a última consoante e acrescentamos ***-er***;
- a adjetivos de uma sílaba terminados em ***-e*** acrescentamos apenas ***-r***;
- no caso de adjetivos de duas sílabas terminados em ***-y***, tiramos o ***-y*** e acrescentamos ***-ier***.

Agora faça as atividades 2 e 3.

COMPARATIVES: EQUALITY

Paris is **as beautiful as** Venice.
(Both are equally beautiful.)
Paris is **not as beautiful as** Venice.
(Venice is more beautiful.)

Quando comparamos dois elementos, indicando que um é igual ao outro, usamos o grau comparativo de igualdade.
- A estrutura deste comparativo é bem simples e vale para qualquer adjetivo: ***as* + adjetivo + *as***.

Importante:
- Quando queremos expressar que algo não é superior ou é inferior a outro, usamos ***not* + *as* + adjetivo + *as***.

Agora faça a atividade 4.

PREPOSITIONS OF PLACE

The ball is **on** the box.

The ball is **next to** the box.

The ball is **between** the boxes.

The ball is **in front of** the box.

The ball is **across from** the box.

The ball is **under** the box.

The ball is **behind** the box.

Agora faça a atividade 5.

SOME, ANY, NO

A: Good afternoon! Would you like **some** water?
B: Yes, I want **some** sparkling water, please. Can I have **some** lemonade, too?
A: Sorry, we **don't** have **any** lemons today.
C: Do you have **any** brownies?
A: Sorry, there are **no** brownies left.

Em inglês, ***some*** significa "um pouco", "algum, alguns". Essa palavra é usada na **afirmativa** e na **interrogativa**, quando queremos **fazer pedidos** ou **oferecer** algo.

Any, por sua vez, é usado na **negativa** e na **interrogativa**. Na interrogativa, a palavra significa ""alguma(s)" ou "algum/alguns". Na negativa, a palavra pode ser traduzida como "nenhum(a)".

A palavra ***no***, por sua vez, é **sinônima de *any***. Contudo, ***any*** é usado na negativa, mas ***no*** (mesmo tendo um sentido negativo) é usado na **afirmativa**, pois não podemos "negar" duas vezes na mesma frase.

Importante:
- Na maioria dos casos, ***some***, ***any*** e ***no*** vêm antes de substantivos.

Agora faça a atividade 6.

Word pop-up

within – dentro de
to overcome – superar
storekeeper – atendente de loja
to lead to – levar a
mists – névoas
to engage – envolver
leading-edge – linha de frente
prejudice – preconceito
to back away – afastar-se
crowded – lotado(a)
toward – em direção a

1 **Unscramble the words used to describe cities, places, and things. Then find them in the wordsearch.**

a. u t r a l l u c — cultural

b. m o l i n a t p o c o s —

c. e l w l – w o n n k —

d. r a t i c t i s —

e. s u o r e m u n —

f. o d n e r m —

g. p u l o o p s u —

h. l a l s m —

i. g b i —

B	X	N	Y	T	J	H	N	P	I	O	Q	K	C	T	M	M	S	O	Z	S	O
G	Y	Q	R	Q	E	N	Q	M	E	X	S	M	S	G	L	G	C	U	A	K	B
T	C	U	L	T	U	R	A	L	P	L	M	J	Z	C	E	F	Y	A	K	E	P
C	J	S	J	O	C	E	H	K	Q	A	A	C	R	E	Z	I	O	I	M	M	P
W	R	A	D	V	B	D	X	U	B	V	L	G	U	B	K	C	Y	V	X	T	P
V	X	V	F	D	M	O	T	P	W	E	L	L	-	K	N	O	W	N	S	I	B
T	C	B	T	L	U	M	Q	E	U	R	Q	O	S	V	O	S	B	E	R	X	I
F	I	S	N	L	B	O	P	D	R	W	H	S	G	Q	N	M	A	G	Z	M	G
U	U	U	Z	H	H	C	Q	B	O	G	X	N	Z	D	A	O	C	V	V	A	O
V	H	S	L	I	Z	E	J	A	D	O	U	M	D	R	L	P	G	P	W	T	C
X	N	U	M	E	R	O	U	S	X	I	S	E	Z	A	C	O	J	I	I	V	U
O	E	W	Q	U	R	E	X	S	R	P	A	P	O	P	U	L	O	U	S	P	T
G	V	A	H	P	J	J	H	U	G	C	M	A	X	R	Y	I	C	A	A	W	R
Q	I	Y	V	Q	E	W	F	A	B	H	N	M	L	Q	O	T	A	T	X	C	O
G	A	R	T	I	S	T	I	C	O	G	Z	Z	D	B	K	A	R	T	J	X	B
K	S	P	K	G	S	V	P	G	S	X	V	K	T	O	H	N	N	F	D	I	E

2 **Complete the table with the correct comparative form. Then match the adjectives to their opposites.**

	Adjective	Comparative
a.	old	older
b.	big	
c.	long	
d.	beautiful	
e.	dangerous	
f.	clean	

- [ ] uglier
- [ ] safer
- [a] younger
- [ ] dirtier
- [ ] smaller
- [ ] shorter

3 Complete the sentences with the comparative form.

a. Edinburgh Castle is older than Windsor Castle. (old)

b. My street is ______ your street. (long)

c. In my opinion, Lisbon is ______ Madrid. (beautiful)

d. A Lhasa Apso dog is ______ a Labrador. (small)

e. Ipanema Beach is ______ Atalaia Beach. (crowded)

f. I think downtown is ______ our neighborhood. (dangerous)

4 Read about the cities. Then write sentences using *as… as* in the affirmative or negative form.

Average temperature: 11 °C
Weather: Strong winds, hot summers, and cold winters
Number of colleges: 5
Seaside beach: No
Population density: 4920 people/km²
Cost of a monthly public transportation ticket: $65
Lakes: Yes

Average temperature: 11.2 °C
Weather: Strong winds, hot summers, and cold winters
Number of colleges: 24
Seaside beach: No
Population density: 4447 people/km²
Cost of a monthly public transportation ticket: $100
Lakes: Yes

a. summer (hot)

Boston is as hot as Chicago in the summer.

b. college (many colleges)

c. population (populous)

d. winter (cold)

e. public transportation ticket (expensive)

f. weather (windy)

5 Look at the picture. Then complete the sentences with a preposition from the box.

in front of
next to
between
~~across from~~
on
behind

a. The bakery is across from the bookstore.

b. The bus stop is ______ the newsstand.

c. The gym is ______ the supermarket and the bank.

d. The cat is ______ the park bench.

e. The man is ______ the cat.

f. The bookstore is ______ the supermarket.

6 Complete with *some*, *any*, or *no*.

a. There aren't any eggs in the fridge.

b. I'd like a hot dog and ______ apple juice.

c. I'm sorry. There are ______ tomatoes today.

d. Are there ______ oranges in the basket?

e. Can I have ______ more water, please?

f. Mom! There's ______ milk left. Can you go to the supermarket and buy ______ milk, please?

iCan

Check (✓) the box that best describes your performance in this unit.

1. I can compare places and things that are different. ☐ Yes, I can. ☐ Not sure.
2. I can compare places and things that are the same. ☐ Yes, I can. ☐ Not sure.
3. I can talk about the position of things. ☐ Yes, I can. ☐ Not sure.
4. I can ask and answer questions using *some*, *any*, and *no*. ☐ Yes, I can. ☐ Not sure.

My city is the coolest!

SUPERLATIVES

Mount Everest is **the highest** mountain in the world. It is 8,848 meters (29,028 feet) high.

Many people say Tokyo is **the most modern** city in the world.

Usamos o superlativo para indicar o grau mais elevado da qualidade de um elemento.

Em inglês, assim como o comparativo de superioridade, formamos esse grau de duas formas:

- com adjetivos de uma sílaba, adicionamos ***-est*** ao final da palavra;
- com adjetivos de duas ou mais sílabas, usamos a seguinte estrutura: ***most* + adjetivo**.

Importante:

- quando o adjetivo tem apenas uma sílaba e termina em **consoante + vogal + consoante** (CVC), dobramos a última consoante e acrescentamos ***-est***, como em ***biggest*** e ***hottest***;
- em adjetivos de uma sílaba terminados em ***-e***, acrescentamos apenas ***-st***, como em ***safest*** e ***nicest***;
- no caso de adjetivos de duas sílabas terminados em ***-y***, tiramos o ***-y*** e acrescentamos ***-iest***, como em ***funniest*** e ***easiest***;
- antes do superlativo, usamos o artigo definido ***the***.

Faça as atividades de 1 a 5.

COMPARATIVES vs. SUPERLATIVES

Ava is **taller than** Zach, but Mike is **the tallest**.

Soccer is **more exciting than** volleyball, but basketball is **the most exciting** sport.

Quando comparamos três ou mais elementos (sejam eles pessoas ou objetos), é comum usarmos tanto o grau comparativo quanto o superlativo.

Nesses casos, utilizamos o comparativo para comparar dois elementos, e o superlativo para indicar aquele que tem a característica mais acentuada.

Importante:

- alguns adjetivos têm formas irregulares tanto no grau comparativo quanto no superlativo. Veja alguns exemplos na tabela a seguir.

Agora faça as atividades 6 e 7.

Irregular Comparative and Superlative Forms

Adjectives	Comparative	Superlative
good	better than	the best
bad	worse than	the worst
far	further/ farther than	the furthest/ farthest

Word pop-up

random – aleatório(a)
illnesses – doenças
newborn – recém-nascido(a)
hunting – caça
dune – dunas
hill – morro, colina
wildlife – vida selvagem

1 Write the superlative forms of these adjectives in the correct columns.

large rich busy tall interesting heavy safe expensive old
dangerous amazing young famous funny nice difficult easy cheap

-st	-est	-iest	most
largest	richest	busiest	interesting

2 Complete the sentences with the superlative forms of the adjectives.

a. The Nile is the longest river in the world. (long)

b. Great Danes are ________ dog breed. (large)

c. The Blue Whale is ________ sea animal. (fat)

d. Patricia always gets good grades in her exams. She is ________ student in my class. (intelligent)

e. I can't play tennis. I am ________ player in my school. (bad)

3 Read and complete the text with the superlative forms of the adjectives.

THE MOST VISITED CITY IN THE WORLD

Bangkok, in Thailand, is the most popular travel destination in the world. What do you know about this place?

Bangkok is the most enigmatic (enigmatic) city in Asia. It is ______ (traditional) and ______ (modern) place in the world at the same time. Traffic is intense, which is why it's considered one of ______ (polluted) places in the world. There are cars and buses, but river taxis and ferries are still ______ (popular) means of transportation. Bangkok is also considered one of ______ (good) places to shop in Asia because it has ______ (low) prices in the world. Bangkok's Chinatown is commonly referred to as ______ (large) in the world. The average temperature in Bangkok is 28 degrees celsius for the entire year, and it's considered one of ______ (hot) cities in the world.

4 Now write sentences about Brazil. Use the superlative form.

a. delicious / food: ______

b. hot / city: ______

c. good / song: ______

d. beautiful / beach: ______

5 Circle the odd one out.

a. difficult hard tough far

b. interesting dangerous amazing beautiful

c. tall short expensive thin

d. young big large huge

6 Who's who in the English class? Look at the picture and read the clues. Then write the names.

Mike

a. Ann has medium-length hair and Greg is thin.
b. Justin's hair is shorter than Greg's.
c. Erica's hair is shorter than Ann's.
d. Both Mike and Justin wear glasses, but Mike's glasses are bigger.
e. Lucas is as tall as Taylor and has brown hair.
f. Erica's hat isn't biggest, and Taylor has the longest hair.
g. Ann's legs are thinner than Erika's.
h. Greg's book is heavier than Lucas' book.

7 Write sentences using the comparative and superlative form. Use the adjectives in parentheses.

a. horse – cow – cheetah (fast)

A horse is faster than a cow, but a cheetah is the fastest.

b. car – bicycle – helicopter (expensive)

c. sea horse – tortoise – sloth (slow)

d. sofa – chair – bed (comfortable)

e. African elephant – brown bear – blue whale (big)

iCan

Check (✓) the box that best describes your performance in this unit.

1. I can describe places, people, and things. ☐ Yes, I can. ☐ Not sure.
2. I can use the comparative form. ☐ Yes, I can. ☐ Not sure.
3. I can use the superlative form. ☐ Yes, I can. ☐ Not sure.

PAST OF *BE*: QUESTIONS

A: Was Mark Zuckerberg born in Canada?
B: No, he wasn't.
A: Where was he born?
B: He was born in the U.S.A.
A: When was he born?
B: He was born on May 14th, 1984.

Affirmative	Negative	Interrogative
Singular	**Singular**	Was I...?
I was	I was not	Was he/she/it...?
You were	You were not	Were we/you/they...?
He/She/It was	He/She/It was not	
Plural	**Plural**	
We/You/They were	We/You/They were not	

Contractions
was not = wasn't were not = weren't

Em inglês, usamos o ***Simple Past*** para falar de ações e estados que se iniciaram e terminaram em um momento definido no passado, que pode ou não estar explícito na frase.

As formas afirmativas do verbo ***to be*** no passado são ***was*** (para ***I***, ***he***, ***she*** e ***it***) e ***were*** (para ***you***, ***we*** e ***they***).

Para formar a negativa, basta acrescentar ***not*** depois de ***to be*** ou usar as contrações ***wasn't*** (***was*** + ***not***) e ***weren't*** (***were*** + ***not***).

Na interrogativa, para fazer ***yes/no questions***, invertemos a ordem entre ***to be*** e o sujeito. Para formar perguntas usando ***question words***, basta inserir a ***question word*** (como ***what*** e ***where***) no início da pergunta. O restante segue a mesma estrutura das ***yes/no questions***.

Importante:
- em respostas negativas a ***yes/no questions***, é mais comum usarmos as formas contraídas de ***to be***;

Agora faça as atividades 1 e 2.

PAST OF *THERE IS/ THERE ARE*

A: Was there a burger place in your grandparents' neighborhood?
B: Yes, **there was**: Joe's burger.

Como já vimos, utilizamos ***there*** + ***be*** para indicar a existência de algo ou alguém. No passado, devemos usar as formas de ***to be*** no ***Simple Past***.

Na negativa, usamos o verbo ***to be*** no ***Simple Past***, seguido de ***not*** ou das contrações ***wasn't*** e ***weren't***.

Para formar a interrogativa, invertemos a ordem entre ***there*** e ***to be***.

Agora faça as atividades 3 e 4.

SIMPLE PAST: REGULAR VERBS

Dad **worked** until late last Tuesday.

Para formarmos a afirmativa do ***Simple Past*** com verbos regulares, ou seja, que seguem uma regra, acrescentamos ***-ed*** ao final da palavra.

Na negativa, para todas as pessoas, usamos o auxiliar ***did*** seguido de ***not*** (ou ***didn't***) e o verbo principal na ***base form***.

Importante:
- em verbos terminados em **consoante** + **vogal** + **consoante** (CVC), dobramos a última consoante e acrescentamos ***-ed***, como em ***stopped*** e ***preferred***. Quando a primeira sílaba do verbo é a tônica, como em ***opened***, não dobramos a consoante na forma do ***Simple Past***.
- no caso de verbos terminados em ***-y*** quando precedido por consoante, tiramos o ***-y*** e acrescentamos ***-ied***, como em ***worried*** e ***tried***.

Agora faça a atividade 5.

SIMPLE PAST: QUESTIONS

A: Did you visit New York on your last vacation?
B: Yes, I **did**. I liked it a lot!

Para formarmos ***yes/no questions*** no ***Simple Past***, usamos o auxiliar ***did*** seguido do ***sujeito*** e do ***verbo*** principal na ***base form***.

Importante:
- em respostas a ***yes/no questions***, podemos usar apenas ***did*** (ou ***didn't***) ou o verbo conjugado no ***Simple Past***;
- sempre que usamos o auxiliar ***did***, o verbo principal fica na ***base form***.

Agora faça as atividades 6 e 7.

Word pop-up

astonishing – surpreendente
speeches – discursos
crowd – multidão
to lead to – levar a

1 Read the profile of Albert Einstein and answer the questions.

Name: Albert Einstein
Birthdate: March 14th, 1879
Birthplace: Ulm, Württemberg, Germany
Occupation: mathematician and physicist
Award: Nobel Prize for Physics in 1921
Discovery: The general theory of relativity

a. When was Einstein born?

He was born on March 14, 1879.

b. Was he born in Austria?

______

c. Was he the winner of the Physics Nobel Prize in 1921?

______

d. Was he an astronomer?

______

e. What was his discovery?

______

2 Read the short biography of the Wright Brothers and complete it with *was* or *were*.

The Wright Brothers
American Aviation Pioneers

These [were] some of the most famous brothers in history. The Wright Brothers [____] leaders in aviation. They [____] responsible for the first plane. Orville Wright [____] born on August 19th, 1871 in Ohio, the U.S.A. Wilbur Wright [____] born on April 16th, 1867 in Indiana, the U.S.A. The two brothers [____] inseparable. Orville [____] full of ideas and Wilbur [____] more mature and better with projects. The Wright brothers [____] the first to complete a man-powered flight in a heavier-than-air machine on December 17th, 1903.

3 Look at the pictures. Then read what each people say and circle the correct form of *there + to be* in the past.

a. Let me tell you how my office was many years ago. **There wasn't/There were** much technology at that time. **There wasn't/There weren't** laptops like today. **There were/There was** a typewriter that I used to write papers. **There were/There wasn't** lots of things made of paper on my desk: a calendar, an envelope, and an appointment book. **There was/There wasn't** a pen, too. **There was/There were** big objects at that time. **There weren't/There was** a big camera to take pictures. And the telephones? Well... **There weren't/There was** small cell phones. In my house, **there wasn't/there were** only corded phones.

Mary Ann, 55

b. This was my office a few years ago. It was different from my mom's office when she was my age. **There weren't/There were** a lot of objects on my desk, but **there was/there were** three electronic devices. **There wasn't/There was** a laptop and **there was/there were** a tablet. They were my favorite! **There was/There wasn't** a camera, too, just like on my mom's desk, but my camera was more modern. **There were/There weren't** lots of papers. In fact, **there wasn't/there was** any paper on my desk. **There was/There wasn't** just a pen. I wear glasses, so **there weren't/there was** always a pair of glasses on my desk. And of course, my cell phone.

Jimmy, 25

4 Unscramble the sentences.

a. Internet / your mom / ? / was a child / there / was / when

Was there Internet when your mom was a child?

b. in my class / was / an American student / there / in 2016 / .

c. weren't / on the streets / many cars / there / in 1950 / .

d. cell phones / ? / were / in 1960 / there

e. in your / was / ? / there / an analog TV / grandmother's house

5 Write these verbs in the Simple Past form.

a. to clean: cleaned	**d.** to chat	**g.** to talk
b. to watch	**e.** to play	**h.** to help
c. to study	**f.** to listen	**i.** to wash

6 Complete the sentences with the Simple Past form of the verbs in parentheses.

a. I didn't listen to music yesterday.
I studied for the science test. (not to listen / to study)

b. Yesterday was a busy day! My sister ________ the dog and I ________ our bedroom. (to walk / to clean)

c. Our parents ________ home last Saturday. They ________ tennis at the club. (not to stay / to play)

d. My friends ________ me last Sunday. We ________ a lot and ________ a movie. (to visit / to chat / to watch)

e. I ________ my mom yesterday. I ________ the house, but I ________ the clothes while she ________ lunch. (to help / not to clean / to wash / to cook)

7 What did you do last weekend? Answer the questions using *Yes, I did* or *No, I didn't*.

a. Did you watch a movie? ________

b. Did you listen to music? ________

c. Did you help your parents with the housework? ________

d. Did you chat with your friends? ________

e. Did you play a sport? ________

f. Did you study for a test? ________

iCan

Check (✓) the box that best describes your performance in this unit.

1. I can use *to be* to talk about past events.	☐ Yes, I can.	☐ Not sure.
2. I can use *there* + *to be* to talk about past facts.	☐ Yes, I can.	☐ Not sure.
3. I can use regular verbs to talk about past events.	☐ Yes, I can.	☐ Not sure.
4. I can ask *yes/no* questions about past events.	☐ Yes, I can.	☐ Not sure.

SIMPLE PAST: IRREGULAR VERBS (AFFIRMATIVE AND NEGATIVE SENTENCES)

Tom **didn't have** lunch at home yesterday. He **had** lunch at school.

Irregular verbs (verbos irregulares) são aqueles que não seguem um padrão para a formação do passado e do particípio. Por isso, às vezes é necessário memorizarmos a forma como são conjugados e, em caso de dúvida, fazer consulta. Você encontrará uma lista desses verbos nas páginas 144 e 145.

Alguns dos ***irregular verbs*** e as respectivas formas no ***Simple Past*** são:

go	***went***
get	***got***
have	***had***
see	***saw***
cut	***cut***
sleep	***slept***
eat	***ate***

SIMPLE PAST: IRREGULAR VERBS (QUESTIONS)

A: Did Doug and Sarah **go** home after school?
B: No, they **didn't**. They **went** running.

A: What **did** Dora **do** yesterday?
B: She **read** a book in the library.

Para formar perguntas no ***Simple Past***, usamos a seguinte estrutura: verbo auxiliar ***did*** + sujeito + verbo principal na ***base form***.

Se quisermos formar ***questions with question words***, basta inserirmos a ***question word*** no início da pergunta. O restante da estrutura permanece igual.

Importante:

- sempre que usamos o auxiliar ***did***, o verbo principal fica na ***base form***.

Agora faça as atividades 1 a 5.

SEQUENCE WORDS

Last weekend was great! **First** I woke up early. **Then** I brushed my teeth and **after that** I went on a picnic in the park with Mom and Dad.

First → Then → After that

Quando contamos uma história, precisamos deixar clara para o ouvinte ou o leitor a ordem em que as coisas aconteceram. Em inglês, empregamos as ***sequence words*** com esse objetivo.

Até agora, você viu as seguintes ***sequence words***:

- ***first***: indica o que aconteceu primeiro;
- ***then***: sinaliza que um evento ocorreu em seguida de outro;
- ***after that***: também expressa a ideia de que um evento aconteceu depois do outro.

Agora faça as atividades 6 e 7.

Word pop-up

arrested for – passado particípio de *to arrest*, preso(a) por
cartridge – cartucho
curfews – recolher obrigatório, toque de recolher
fall – queda
hired – particípio passado de *to hire*, contratado(a)
huge – enorme(s)
reached – passado de *to reach*, atingiu
world affairs – assuntos mundiais
fixed – passado de *to fix*, preparei
slave – escravo(a)
fern – samambaia

1 Use the verbs in the past to complete the conversation.

to read | ~~to have~~ | to go | to ride | to eat | to hang out

Anna: Hi, Caio! How are you?

Caio: I'm fine, but I'm tired. I had a busy day yesterday.

Anna: Really? What did you do?

Caio: I ________ to the club in the morning and ________ my bike.

Anna: What did you do in the afternoon?

Caio: I ________ with some friends and we ________ pizza at the mall.

Anna: Wow! You did a lot! Did you go to bed early?

Caio: No, I didn't. I ________ my favorite book for two hours before going to bed.

2 Write affirmative (+) or negative sentences (-) using the Simple Past. Follow the example.

a. Eddie / wake up / late / yesterday. (+)

Eddie woke up late yesterday.

b. Barbara / help / me / with my homework. (-)

____

c. My parents and I / eat / pasta for lunch / last Sunday. (+)

____

d. Luana / hang out with friends / and go to the movies. (+)

____

3 What did Doug do yesterday? Write sentences following the example.

a. to read He didn't read a magazine. He read a book.

____

b. to make ________

____

c. to eat ________

____

4 Read the Garfield comic about what happened yesterday. Then check (✓) the correct answer.

a. Did Garfield go to the movies yesterday?
- [ ] Yes, he did. - [x] No, he didn't.

b. Did Garfield watch TV?
- [ ] Yes, he did. - [ ] No, he didn't.

c. Did Bob see the movie?
- [ ] Yes, he did. - [ ] No, he didn't.

d. What did Bob do during the movie?
- [ ] He slept. - [ ] He left the room.

e. Did Garfield like Bob's answer?
- [ ] Yes, he did. - [ ] No, he didn't.

5 Look at the pictures. Then read the sentences and write *B* for Bruno or *M* for Malala.

Bruno Mars, singer

Malala Yousafzai, Pakistani activist

a. This person hung out with friends. M

b. This person ate chicken for lunch. ____

c. This person watched sports on TV. ____

d. This person drank orange juice. ____

e. This person read a book. ____

f. This person played a musical instrument. ____

g. This person ate pizza for dinner. ____

h. This person listened to music. ____

6 Look at the pictures. Then number the events (1-5) to form a story.

Then he put up a tent. [ ]

After chopping wood he cooked some food. [ ]

Jake went camping last week. [1]

After that he chopped wood. [ ]

First he packed his things. [ ]

7 Look at the pictures and write a story. Use *first*, *then*, and *after that*.

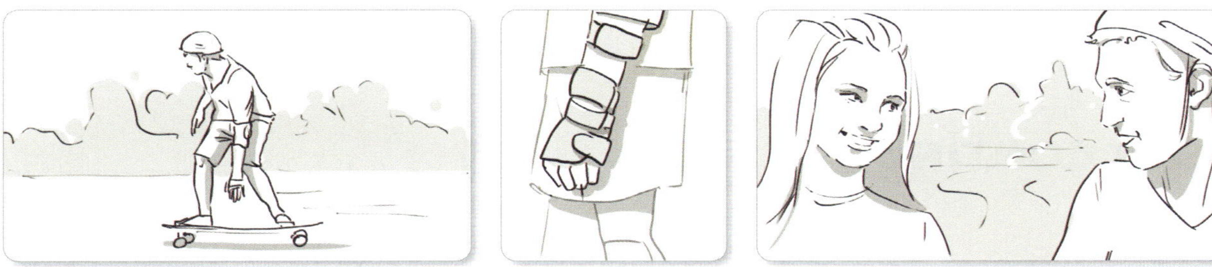

It was a sunny day at the park. Pedro…

iCan

Check (✓) the box that best describes your performance in this unit.

1. I can use irregular verbs to talk about past events.	[ ] Yes, I can.	[ ] Not sure.
2. I can use *did* and *didn't* to talk about the past.	[ ] Yes, I can.	[ ] Not sure.
3. I can ask *Yes/No* questions about past events.	[ ] Yes, I can.	[ ] Not sure.
4. I can use sequence words to talk about past events and tell a story.	[ ] Yes, I can.	[ ] Not sure.

What did you do last night?

SIMPLE PAST: QUESTIONS

A: Did you sleep at Rick's place yesterday?
B: No, I **didn't**.
A: Where did you sleep?
B: I **slept** at Jordan's. We played video games until late.

Como você viu na unidade anterior, para formar ***yes/no questions*** no ***Simple Past***, usamos ***did*** e o sujeito e verbo principal na ***base form***.

As perguntas com ***question words*** são formadas com a ***question word*** no início da pergunta. O restante da estrutura continua igual à das ***yes/no questions***.

Importante:

- nas respostas as ***yes/no questions***, geralmente usamos apenas o verbo auxiliar ***did*** ou a contração da sua forma negativa (***didn't***);
- as perguntas com ***question words***, em contrapartida, pedem uma resposta completa.

Agora faça as atividades 1 e 2.

PAST CONTINUOUS

Monica **was** check**ing** her e-mails at 6 a.m.

Em inglês, usamos o ***Past Continuous*** para expressar ações que estavam em progresso, acontecendo no passado.

Formar esse tempo verbal é bem simples.

Na afirmativa, usamos o ***Simple Past*** do verbo ***to be*** (***was*** para ***I***, ***he***, ***she*** e ***it***; e ***were*** para ***we***, ***you*** e ***they***) seguido do verbo principal com ***-ing***.

Para formar a negativa, utilizamos a forma verbal ***was*** ou ***were*** seguida de ***not*** ou as formas contraídas ***wasn't*** e ***weren't***.

Agora faça a atividade 3.

PAST CONTINUOUS: QUESTIONS

A: Were you **doing** your homework at 4 p.m. yesterday?
B: No, I **wasn't**.
A: What **were** you **doing**?
B: I **was cleaning** my room.

Para fazer ***yes/no questions*** no ***Past Continuous***, invertemos a ordem entre o sujeito e o verbo ***to be*** no ***Simple Past***. O verbo principal permanece com ***-ing***.

Formamos as ***questions with question words*** com as ***question words*** que iniciam a pergunta. Depois delas, a estrutura continua a mesma: verbo ***to be*** no ***Simple Past*** + sujeito + verbo principal com ***-ing***.

Importante:

- Nós respondemos a ***yes/no questions*** apenas com o verbo ***to be***, sem o verbo principal. Na negativa, usamos as formas contraídas do verbo ***to be*** (***wasn't*** e ***weren't***).

Agora faça a atividade 4.

PAST CONTINUOUS vs. SIMPLE PAST

Robert **was studying** when his sister **arrived** home.
When Robert's sister **arrived** home, he **was studying**.
OR
Robert's sister **arrived** home while he **was studying**.
While Robert **was studying**, his sister **arrived** home.

É comum utilizarmos, na mesma frase, o ***Simple Past*** e o ***Past Continuous***. Nesses casos, usamos o ***Past Continuous*** para indicar a ação que estava em andamento e o ***Simple Past*** para expressar o acontecimento que interrompeu a ação que estava acontecendo.

Importante:

- ***When***: usamos para indicar que um evento ocorreu em algum momento no passado. Empregamos essa conjunção geralmente antes de orações com o ***Simple Past***.
- ***While***: utilizamos para indicar uma ação em progresso que foi interrompida por outra. Normalmente, ele introduz a oração em que está o verbo no ***Past Continuous***.

Agora faça as atividades 5 e 6.

Word pop-up

stood up for – passado de *to stand up for*, defendeu
laureate – ganhador(a)
refused – passado de *to refuse*, recusou
tale – história, relato, conto
ultimate – final
uprooted – particípio passado de *to uproot*, desenraizado(a)
was shot – foi baleado(a)
earthquake – terremoto
homeless – sem teto
dust – pó
barely – mal

1 Read Luca's blog post about a trip to Paris. Then match the questions and answers.

Luca's Blog

My first visit to Paris was unforgettable. It was a great feeling to arrive and see the city of light, which is both modern and rich in history.

In the evening, the city was lit up with Christmas lights. My family and I went to see the Opera house and then walked to Place de la Concorde.

Later, we got hungry since it was late. We decided to eat at a Lebanese restaurant near the Champs-Élysées.

We were staying in Épinay-sur-Seine, which is 11.3 km north from the center of Paris.

The next morning, we explored the small town. Since it was Christmas Day, all the shops were closed.

We spent ten days in Paris and had an amazing time.

a. How was Luca's experience in Paris?
b. Where did he have dinner?
c. Where were they staying?
d. Were the shops open on Christmas Day?
e. When did they travel to Paris?
f. How long did he stay in Paris?

[ ] He had dinner in a Lebanese restaurant.
[ ] He stayed there for ten days.
[ ] They were staying in the north of Paris.
[a] It was amazing.
[ ] No, they were closed.
[ ] They traveled at Christmas time.

2 Unscramble the questions and answer them writing about you.

a. did you / vacation / ? / What / on your / do / last

What did you do on your last vacation? | ______

b. go / you / did /? / Where

______ | ______

c. you / ? / read / Did / a book

______ | ______

d. to the movies / Did / you / ? / go

______ | ______

e. What time / wake up / ? / you / did

______ | ______

3 Look at the pictures. What were these people doing last Saturday at 3 p.m.? Use the verbs in the box to write sentences in the Past Continuous.

to watch TV	to walk	to do yoga	to rollerblade	to play soccer	~~to read a book~~	to walk the dog	to shop

Lucy and Tim

They were reading a book.

McMurphy family

Brenda

Paulo

Daniel

Monica

Clara

Mr. and Mrs. Thompson

4 Write dialogues for the prompts below.

a. play soccer **X** take selfies

A: Were you playing soccer at 4 p.m. yesterday?

B: No, I wasn't.

A: Then what were you doing?

B: I was taking selfies.

b. make the bed **X** make a shower

A: ______ at 7 a.m.?

B: No, I ______.

A: Then what ______?

B: I ______.

c. listen to music **X** study for a test

A: ______ on Saturday afternoon?

B: No, we ______.

A: Then what ______?

B: We ______.

d. play volleyball **X** text a friend

A: ______ he ______ yesterday morning?

B: No, he ______.

A: Then what ______?

B: He ______ a friend.

e. cooking dinner **X** watching TV

A: ______ she ______ at 8 p.m. last night?

B: No, she ______.

A: Then what ______?

B: She ______ TV.

5 Complete the story using *when* or *while*.

Camila is a student at Laurel Middle School. Yesterday she was at the library [when] something really strange happened. [ ] she was looking for a book on the shelves at the back, she heard someone whispering her name. She looked around, but there was no one there. [ ] she came back to her desk, she heard someone calling her name again. She was scared. [ ] she was packing her things and leaving, she heard a noise. It was her cell phone vibrating. There was a text message from Sophia that said: 'Camila, help me! The bathroom door won't open. I am locked inside.' 'Phew!' she thought. 'What a relief! So that was the voice I was hearing!'

6 Complete the sentences using the Simple Past or the Past Continuous.

a. He [was riding] a bike when he [fell down]. (to ride/to fall down)

b. While she [ ] a movie, she [ ]. (to watch/to fall asleep)

c. The students [ ] loudly when the principal [ ]. (to talk/to arrive)

d. Vinicius [ ] a text message when he [ ] into the wall. (to send/to walk)

e. I [ ] on the phone when my mom [ ] home. (to talk/to get)

f. He [ ] his nose while he [ ] volleyball. (to break/to play)

iCan

Check (✓) the box that best describes your performance in this unit.

1. I can talk about past vacation activities. ☐ Yes, I can. ☐ Not sure.

2. I can talk about past actions. ☐ Yes, I can. ☐ Not sure.

3. I can use the Past Continuous to talk about past events. ☐ Yes, I can. ☐ Not sure.

4. I can describe an action that happened while another action was going on. ☐ Yes, I can. ☐ Not sure.

Are you feeling better?

REQUESTS: *CAN* AND *COULD*

A: Dad, **can** we **listen** to this vinyl record?
B: Sure!

A: Mr. Byrne, **could** we **do** the test next week?
B: Sorry, Michael, you **can't**. You and your classmates have to do it tomorrow.

Em inglês, usamos ***can*** para fazer pedidos informalmente.

Podemos usar também a forma ***could***, mas para fazer pedidos em situações mais formais.

Para formar perguntas com ***can*** e ***could***, basta inverter a posição entre eles e o sujeito.

Importante:
- usamos as expressões ***sure*** e ***of course*** para conceder pedidos ou concordar em fazer um favor. Elas enfatizam que estamos dispostos a fazer o que foi pedido;
- quando não queremos ou não podemos atender a um pedido ou fazer um favor, usamos a palavra ***sorry***. Além de ser um pedido de desculpas, ela expressa gentileza e boas maneiras.

Agora faça a atividade 1.

ADVICE: *SHOULD*

Mr. Davis, you **should drink** more water and **shouldn't sleep** for less than 8 hours per night.

Em inglês, usamos ***should*** para dar conselhos. Na negativa, usamos ***should not*** ou a contração ***shouldn't***.

Essas formas valem para todas as pessoas do discurso. Depois de ***should***, ***should not*** ou ***shouldn't***, utilizamos o verbo na ***base form***.

Agora faça as atividades 2, 3 e 4.

LIKE, *LOVE*, AND *HATE* + GERUND

Janice **hates** watch**ing** romantic movies, but she **likes** watch**ing** sports programs.

O ***gerund*** é formado com ***verbo*** + ***-ing***. Ele tem o valor de substantivo e é usado depois de verbos como ***like***, ***love*** e ***hate***, desempenhando o papel de objeto.

Importante:
- cuidado para não confundir o uso do gerúndio com o ***-ing*** que usamos após verbos no ***Present*** e no ***Past Continuous***, que indicam uma ação em progresso. Basta lembrar que os verbos nesse tempo sempre são antecedidos de ***to be***, o que não ocorre com o ***gerund***.

Agora faça a atividade 5.

SO AS A CONSEQUENCE

Because it was sunny, the Fullers decided to go to the beach.
↓ **reason** ↓ **consequence**

It was sunny, so the Fullers decided to go to the beach.
↓ **reason** ↓ **consequence**

Em inglês, ***so*** é usado no início de uma oração e estabelece uma relação de consequência entre ela e a outra oração.

Importante:
- ***because*** também introduz orações, expressando a causa de um evento. Quando usamos essa palavra, não utilizamos ***so*** e vice-versa.

Agora faça a atividade 6.

Word pop-up

instead of – ao invés de
weight – peso
loss – perda
booster – amplificador
flavorful – saboroso

1 Match the requests to the correct reply.

a. Could you bring me a glass of water?
b. Can you give me a ride?
c. Can you open the window, please?
d. Can you lend me a blue pen?
e. Could you lend me an umbrella?
f. Can you turn on the lights, please?

[ ] I'm sorry. I'm not driving today. I'm taking the bus.
[a] Sure. Would you like it cold or room temperature?
[ ] Sorry, I can't. The air-conditioning is on.
[ ] Sorry. I don't have one.
[ ] Sure. I'll turn them on.
[ ] Sure! I'm using only one pen now.

2 Write the name of the health problems. Then find them in the wordsearch.

a.
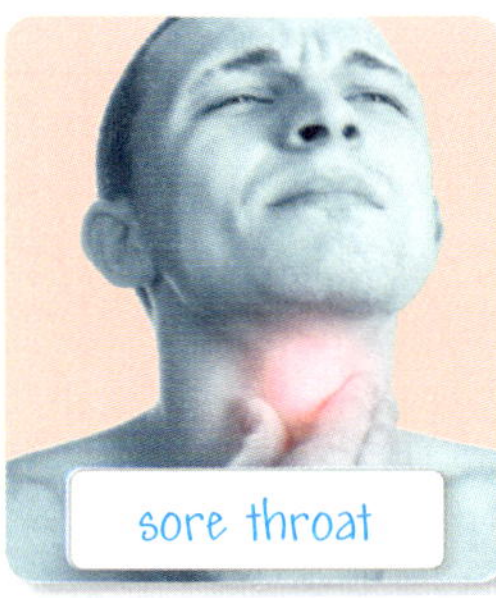

c.
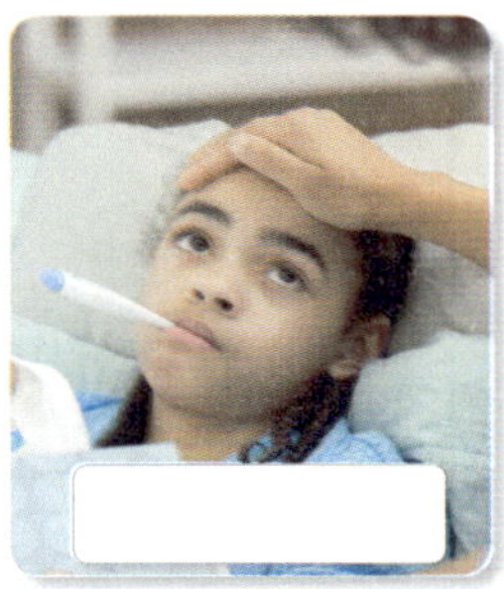

e.

g.

b.
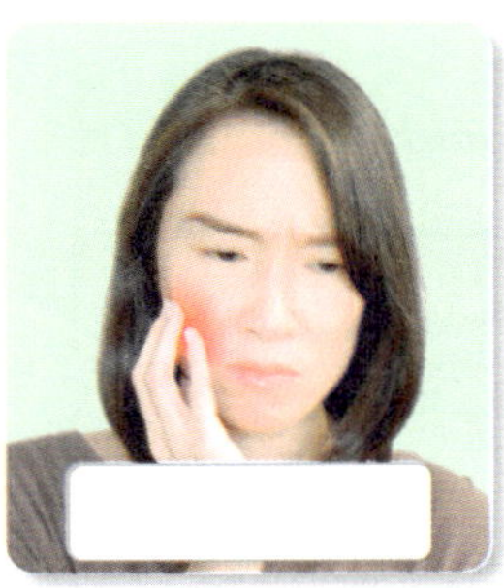

d.

f.
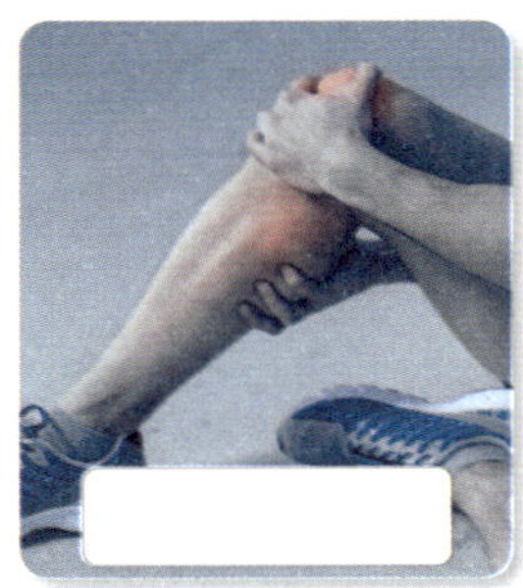

h.
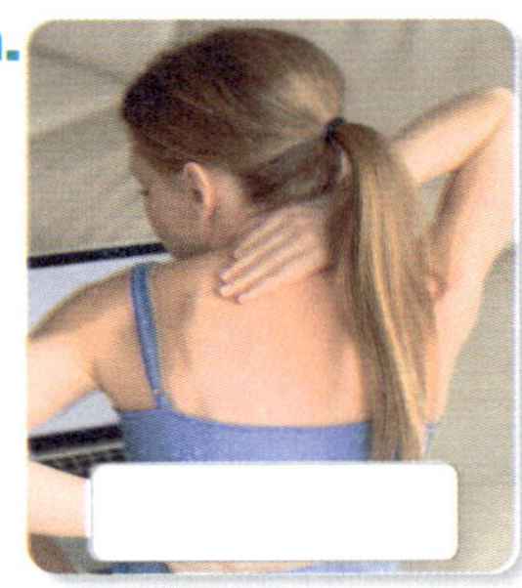

T	R	P	A	I	N	I	N	T	H	E	B	A	C	K	O	M	Z	H	M
O	P	S	Y	B	U	T	T	J	K	D	C	O	H	F	C	W	P	Q	A
O	E	H	C	A	H	C	A	M	O	T	S	B	A	F	E	V	E	R	K
T	W	E	D	F	U	V	X	M	O	M	D	K	M	M	O	I	E	M	R
H	S	A	A	W	S	O	R	E	T	H	R	O	A	T	P	Z	R	N	X
A	A	D	U	F	A	S	V	X	U	C	M	J	V	R	K	P	T	B	F
C	D	A	Y	P	X	E	W	D	H	G	F	D	R	V	Y	A	B	W	T
H	B	C	N	F	M	T	Q	Q	U	K	D	Y	F	I	H	I	W	N	Y
E	U	H	K	Y	F	M	R	S	H	O	A	W	P	U	S	N	E	D	Z
Y	J	E	L	A	N	s	Q	P	Z	H	B	K	B	Y	C	O	L	D	Y

3 Read the comics and answer T (true) or F (false).

a. Snoopy has a headache. F

b. Woodstock is sick.

c. Woodstock should see the vet.

d. Peppermint Pattie has a headache now.

e. She has a stomachache.

f. Marcie tells Pattie she should go home.

4 Use the phrases in the box to give advice to these people using *should* or *shouldn't*.

go to the doctor	save money to buy a new one	~~sit down and rest~~	play video games today

a. **A:** What's the matter?
B: My leg hurts.
A: You should sit down and rest.

b. **A:** What's the matter?
B: I have a lot of homework for tomorrow.
A: ____________________.

c. **A:** What's the matter?
B: I have a fever.
A: ____________________.

d. **A:** What's the matter?
B: My cell phone isn't working.
A: ____________________.

5 Complete the posts on the social media using the gerund of the verbs in parentheses.

I love playing (to play) basketball in my free time.

10 | 3

a. I like ______ (to play) basketball, too.

b. I don't like ______ (to play) sports.

c. I love ______ (to do) gymnastics.

d. I love ______ (to hang out) with my friends.

e. I don't like ______ (to swim) in my free time. I like ______ (to read) online magazines.

6 Rewrite these sentences using *so*.

a. Because we have free tickets, we are going to the rock concert.

We have free tickets, so we are going to the rock concert.

b. Because I have plenty of time, I am going to help you with your homework.

______

c. Because she is not feeling well, I am taking her to the hospital.

______

d. Because I have a test tomorrow, I'm not going to watch TV today.

______

iCan

Check (✓) the box that best describes your performance in this unit.

1. I can make requests using *can* and *could*. ☐ Yes, I can. ☐ Not sure.

2. I can talk about health problems and give advice using *should*. ☐ Yes, I can. ☐ Not sure.

3. I can talk about what I like and don't like doing. ☐ Yes, I can. ☐ Not sure.

4. I can use *so* and *because* to talk about consequences. ☐ Yes, I can. ☐ Not sure.

Audioscripts

Welcome Unit

Loading 1, page 10

Hi guys. This is what I do on Mondays. Monday is a very busy day. I get up at 6 o'clock, have breakfast and then I ride my bike to school. School ends at 3:00 p.m. and then I go to my acting class. I want to be an actor when I'm older. After acting class I go home, I do my homework and at 7:00 p.m. I go to the kitchen to help my mom with dinner. After dinner I usually play video games or watch TV.

Unit 1

Uploading 4, page 17

Anderson: So, Laura… what are you going to do this weekend?

Laura: Well, on Saturday morning, I'm going to study for the Spanish test…

Anderson: Oh, are you going to study? I'm not! On Saturday morning I'm going to enjoy the beach with some friends, and in the afternoon I'm going to the mall.

Laura: Well you should study too; this test is going to be difficult.

Anderson: You're right, maybe on Sunday. What are you going to do on Saturday afternoon?

Laura: I'm going to visit my grandma and after that my cousins and I are going to see a movie.

Anderson: Oh, maybe we can all go to the movies together.

Laura: Cool! My dad is going to meet us after the movie. We're going to have a pizza together.

Anderson: Great! See you then!

iListen 1, page 24

Mother: So, Samantha... What are you going to do this weekend?

Samantha: Well, on Saturday morning I'm going to play basketball at school.

Mother: Again?

Samantha: Yes, Mom, our game is on Monday. We have to practice.

Mother: OK. What about Saturday afternoon?

Samantha: On Saturday afternoon, we are all going to the sports club.

Mother: Great! It's summer. You have to enjoy the swimming pools!

Samantha: I'm not going to swim, Mom! I'm going to play basketball.

Mother: But you're going to play basketball all Saturday long?

Samantha: Yes, Mom. I am!

Mother: Are you going to play basketball on Sunday, too?

Samantha: No. On Sunday I'm going to stay at home and have fun with you guys!

Mother: Perfect! Let's have a picnic then.

Unit 2

Uploading 5, page 31

a. **A:** What will happen to schools in the future?

B: Well, I think robots and teachers will work together in schools.

A: Do you really think so?

b. **A:** The soccer game is on TV tonight. The cup final!

B: You're right! I'll make us some popcorn.

A: Cool!

c. **A:** I'm so thirsty!

B: I'll bring you some water.

A: Thanks.

d. **A:** Will people use smartphones in the year 3000?

B: Of course they will. Smartphones will be very different, but still very popular.

A: Well, I'm not so sure about that.

iListen 1, page 38

1. **A:** Oh… This math exercise is so difficult. I can't do it.

B: Don't worry. I'll help you.

2. **A:** Wow… It's really cold in here. I'm freezing.

B: Hold on. I'll close the window.

3. **A:** I can't answer the phone, Mia. I'm cooking.

B: It's OK. I'll answer it.

4. **A:** I can't text Anna. My cell phone isn't working.

B: I'll text her.

5. **A:** I'm very, very hungry.

B: I'll buy you a sandwich.

6. **A:** I can't understand this text. These words are very difficult.

B: I'll get you a dictionary.

Unit 3

Uploading 5, page 47

Mumbai is the most crowded city in India, with a population of about 20 million people. It is the commercial and financial capital of the country, and is home to many multinational companies and some universities. The weather in July is very rainy, because it is monsoon season, and very dry from January to April. The architecture in Mumbai is a mixture of modern and ancient buildings and like any other big city, it can sometimes be noisy and dirty.

iListen 1, page 54

A: Why don't we go to Brazil on our backpacking trip?

B: Brazil? I don't know much about the places there.

A: Let's have a look in this magazine. There are lots of articles about it. Look at this place. It's called Foz do Iguaçu.

B: Let me see… Wow, it's beautiful! The waterfalls look fantastic.

A: Yes, and there are a lot of other tourist attractions, too. There is a lot more you can see at the National Park.

B: Sounds great! What's the weather like there?

A: It's hot in the summer and January is summer in Brazil, so it will be great.

B: I don't know. Why don't we go to a more historical place… like Machu Picchu, in Peru?

A: Oh, really? Well, that's very different from Foz do Iguaçu…

B: I know. The ruins of the Inca city are so interesting. They're ancient, too. Look at this flyer. We can hike from Cuzco to the city! It's a four-day hike…

A: Hmm… it looks dangerous to me. Look at those mountains…. And it says here it can be very rainy there in January.

B: Well, that could be a problem…

A: I think we need some time to make up our minds…

B: Sure. We'll have a great trip whatever we choose.

Unit 4

iListen 3, page 68

a. **A:** I really can't decide on what to wear for the party tonight.

B: Why don't you wear that pink dress?

A: The pink dress is OK, but I think the blue one is more beautiful.

B: Oh, no, Priscilla… the black dress is the most beautiful one.

A: Yeah, you're right. I'll wear the black dress, then.

b. **A:** It's Mom's birthday on Tuesday! We need to get her a gift.

B: I know! I think we should get her new shoes!

A: That's a good idea… but shoes are expensive. We don't have money for that.

B: Hmm… we could buy her a new bag.

A: No way! Bags are more expensive than shoes. I think we'll only have money for… some chocolate.

B: I guess you're right. Let's buy her some chocolate then. She'll understand.

c. **A:** Hi! We're doing a survey about sports… Can I ask you some questions?

B: Sure!

A: Great. What do you think about surfing?

B: Oh, it is a very dangerous sport , but it's my favorite.

A: Really? What about skateboarding? Do you like it?

B: Skateboarding? It's even more dangerous. I don't really like it. The sea is way better.

A: Oh, I see… how about bungee jumping then?

B: No way! It's the most dangerous sport. I'd never do that!

A: Oh, OK… Thank you for your answers.

Unit 5

iListen 3, page 84

1. She was an English novelist who wrote novels criticizing the British landed gentry at the end of the 18th century. Some of her most famous novels, including *Pride and Prejudice* and *Sense and Sensibility*, are considered literary classics, bridging the gap between romance and realism.

2. He is hugely popular around the world for creating a new genre in art – surrealism. He was passionate about style, statement making, and luxury. He was an excellent draftsman who produced skilled technical drawings.

Unit 6

iListen 3, page 98

A: Hi, Rihanna. What's up?

B: Hey, there! How are you?

A: I'm good… How was your weekend?

B: It was great.

A: Really? What did you do?

B: You know, weekends are usually boring here, but last weekend my family and I went to the beach!

A: Sounds cool! What did you do there?

B: Well, we got up early to go to the beach. First, I walked a lot with my mom and I swam in the ocean. Then at lunchtime, we ate fish and had ice cream. In the afternoon, we played volleyball with some friends we made.

A: That's great!

B: And in the evening we had dinner at The Sixties and played cards.

A: You sound really happy!

Unit 8

iListen 2, page 128

Mr. Wilson: What's the matter, Aaron?

Aaron: I have a stomachache, Mr. Wilson.

Mr. Wilson: You shouldn't play soccer then.

Aaron: I know. But I need to practice. We have an important game tomorrow… Ouch!

Mr. Wilson: I think you should go home and rest. Then tomorrow you will feel better and will be able play.

Aaron: I think you are right… Could you please help me go to the nurse's office?

Mr. Wilson: Sure!

Aaron: Thanks, Mr. Wilson.

Mr. Wilson: You're welcome, Aaron!

Audio tracks

iLearn 3 Student's Book

Unit	section	page	track
	Copyright notice	-	1
Welcome	Loading #1	10	2
Welcome	Loading #2	10	3
Welcome	Loading #1	12	4
Welcome	Loading #3	12	5
Welcome	Loading #3	12	6
1	Loading #1	16	7
1	Uploading #4	17	8
1	Loading #1	18	9
1	Loading #1	20	10
1	Loading #3	20	11
1	Loading #1	22	12
1	iListen #1	24	13
2	Loading #1	30	14
2	Loading #3	30	15
2	Uploading #5	31	16
2	Loading #1	32	17
2	Loading #3	32	18
2	Loading #1	34	19
2	Loading #3	34	20
2	iListen #1	38	21
3	Loading #1	46	22
3	Uploading #5	47	23
3	Loading #1	48	24
3	Loading #3	48	25
3	Loading #1	50	26
3	Loading #3	50	27
3	Loading #1	52	28
3	iListen #1	54	29
4	Loading #1	60	30
4	Loading #1	62	31
4	Loading #3	62	32
4	Loading #1	64	33
4	Loading #3	64	34
4	Loading #1	66	35
4	Loading #3	66	36
4	iListen	68	37
5	Loading #1	76	38
5	Loading #1	78	39
5	Loading #1	80	40
5	Loading #1	82	41
5	Loading #3	82	42
5	iListen #3	84	43
6	Loading #1	90	44
6	Uploading #4	93	45
6	Loading #1	96	46
6	Loading #3	96	47
6	iRead #1	98	48
6	iListen #3	98	49
7	Loading #1	106	50
7	Loading #3	106	51
7	Loading #1	108	52
7	Loading #3	108	53
7	iRead #2	114	54
8	Loading #1	120	55
8	Loading #3	120	56
8	Loading #4	120	57
8	Loading #1	122	58
8	Loading #3	123	59
8	Loading #5	123	60
8	Loading #1	124	61
8	Loading #1	126	62
8	Loading #2	126	63
8	iListen #2	128	64

Notes

Notes

Notes

Notes